Changing to Charter

Changing to Charter

How and Why School Leaders Convert

Rebecca A. Shore, Maria M. Leahy,
and Joel E. Medley

ROWMAN & LITTLEFIELD
Lanham • Boulder • New York • London

Published by Rowman & Littlefield
A wholly owned subsidiary of The Rowman & Littlefield Publishing Group, Inc.
4501 Forbes Boulevard, Suite 200, Lanham, Maryland 20706
www.rowman.com

6 Tinworth Street, London SE11 5AL, United Kingdom

Copyright © 2020 by Rebecca A. Shore, Maria M. Leahy, Joel E. Medley

All rights reserved. No part of this book may be reproduced in any form or by any electronic or mechanical means, including information storage and retrieval systems, without written permission from the publisher, except by a reviewer who may quote passages in a review.

British Library Cataloguing in Publication Information Available

Library of Congress Control Number: 2020940706

ISBN: 978-1-4758-5756-6 (cloth : alk. paper)
ISBN: 978-1-4758-5757-3 (pbk. : alk. paper)
ISBN: 978-1-4758-5758-0 (electronic)

To All Leaders and Learners,
Especially,
Lily, Bobby, and Lily's Bobby,
Alessondra, Lucia, Josie, Ella Mae, and Mila Kate,
Brandt, Campbell, Braxton, and Dawson.

Contents

Acknowledgments		ix
Introduction		1
PART I: NUTS AND BOLTS OF CHANGING TO CHARTER		**5**
1	Charter Schools Defined	7
2	Why Change to Charter?	15
PART II: JOURNEYS OF ADVENTUROUS LEADERS		**25**
3	New Kids on the Block: Vaughn Next Century Learning Center, 2004	27
4	New Leaders on the Block: Vaughn Next Century Learning Center, 2019	49
5	Clawing Your Way	57
6	Success Is a Journey, Not a Destination	65
7	A District School: Feaster-Edison Charter School	75
8	Strengthening Unlikely Partnerships: A School District, a District Charter, and Their Community	87
9	Shared Pain: The Story of Orange Grove Elementary	93
10	A 100-Year Love Story	99

11	What If? A History of the Learning Center! Charter School	107
12	An Island Story	115
13	Legacy of Leadership: The Key to Conversion	125

About the Authors   127

Acknowledgments

As I enter my fortieth year in the education profession I can scarcely contain my gratitude to each and every student and professional whose journey my path has crossed; Leaders, learners, readers, writers, they all, as I, have been driven by a quest to improve learning for all, and I am thankful to share this great adventure of life with so many other truth seekers. The joy of a long career in the education field cannot be matched, and I am thankful for the choice my loving and always supportive parents allowed me to make in becoming a teacher. Choice matters for each of us, and charter schools provide educational choices: oftentimes to those who have few others. Special recognition at the moment goes out to those courageous trailblazers who have started charter schools or changed to charter, particularly those who shared their incredible stories with us to make this book possible. You took big risks, and they all paid off for children, families, and the field of education. Thank you for changing to charter.

First, my thanks go out to Tom Koerner and Carlie Wall at Roman & Littlefield Publishing who have gently and encouragingly guided and assisted me through the production of five books, all of which were high points as I reflect on my career over time. Their life's work at R&L is quite literally getting the word(s) out, shining bright lights of intellectual inquiry on a multitude of complex problems to find possible solutions for us in the field. Thank you, Tom and Carlie and all of the folks at R&L, for your generosity of time and talent toward betterment.

Secondly, to my two coauthors on this particular work; both Maria and Joel were absolutely brilliant former students of mine whose questions captured my thinking and catapulted my imagination. Both were (and are) insightful, kind, curious, hard-working, and amazing. We share core values that transcend time and place. I have learned so much from both of them and am grateful for the results of the crisscrossing of our lifelong ties.

To all my colleagues at UNC Charlotte for your support of my work, especially Bob, Claudia, Cathy, Chuang, Dawson, Debra, Florence, Jamie, Jae Hoon, Jillian, Jim(s), Laurie, Lisa(s), Mark, Mickey, Rich, Ryan, Sandra, Stella, Beth, Alan, Ayesha, Walter, Xiaoxia, and *all* of you from the Department of Educational Leadership and Cato College of Education who engage in meaningful scholarship with optimism, open minds, verve, and a spirit of service! To my inner circle who endure my rants and raves and enrich my life with your friendship and honesty; Tricia, Kathleen, Kim, Robyn (and all of your children and sidekicks). To musical Mara, motivating Lori, awesome Amy, and joyful Jeanette: you know full well I couldn't get through a single week without you.

Finally, to my own family, all of whom bless me beyond measure, beyond expression through words; Bruce, Wynona, Marcus, Lily, Bobby, Melissa, Jenny (and my extensive extended family); I thank you and love you with my whole heart always.

Rebecca A. Shore

Introduction

Changing to Charter is the third in a series of books that are the result of two decades of study of successful, sustained charter school leadership in schools across the United States. The first book, *Adventures of Charter School Creators: Leading from the Ground Up* (2004), examined leadership characteristics of those bold enough to imagine, create, and successfully lead schools within the new (and controversial) educational reform initiative.

Who were those leaders and why and how did they accomplish such success over a decade of school leadership? All chose to embark on their journeys to improve the lives of the underserved and generally poor, and all experienced unusual success over time and thus became our focus of study. Some were school leaders; others had never worked in a school before. We gleaned their lessons of charter school development through the interwoven fabric of (1) the lenses of the unique leaders themselves, (2) the resulting successful organizations which they created, and (3) the environments in which they were built.

In the second book, *Journeys of Charter School Creators: Leadership for the Long Haul* (2019), we followed up with these original leaders, now two decades into their work, and circled back to check in and see how their journeys had progressed since their initial adventures. What had changed? What hadn't? Who were they now and what were they doing? Some of what we learned can be summarized in a paragraph of that book's Preface by Guilbert Hentschke, dean emeritus of the Rossier School of Education at the University of Southern California:

> Case after case, these charter school founders have stayed close to the schools they created and to the communities they served. What they tended not to do is transfer to another school or district and "move on" in a quest for professional

advancement elsewhere. The opportunity structure provided by charter school legislation afforded them a precious (to them) chance to fulfill a dream of creating "their" school. It played into classic entrepreneurial traits. But, in creating their charter schools, they were also captured by them. (xv)

This third book, *Changing to Charter*, zeros in on a subcategory of the original group of leaders, those who started out many years ago as traditional public or private school principals, but then made a decision to change their schools to public charter school status. Why did they "convert" and what have they learned from their experiences that could be shared with others considering making such a change?

This group, by nature, represented a somewhat different breed of risk-taker who had to be prepared to "pick a fight" with their local districts in the case of traditional public school conversions, or their congregations or other sponsoring entities in the case of privates, in the name of improved learning environments on behalf of their constituencies, the students and families, and the schools they served.

As *Journeys of Charter School Creators* was based in part on prior stories shared in *Adventures of Charter School Creators*, so does *Changing to Charter* begin with the initial start-up stories of those leaders who were already in place as school leaders prior to conversion, followed by chapters updating the stories of three of those leaders from the original *Adventures* book.

For example, in the first book, and featured in this one, Yvonne Chan of Vaughn Next Century Learning Center shares her adventures converting her school to charter status. After experiencing the death of a student who was murdered in front of her poorly performing Los Angeles public school in the early 1990s, Chan's frustration with the bureaucratic school system emboldened her. She, along with a group of likeminded individuals, converted her large, failing public elementary school within the Los Angeles Unified School District to charter status and both she, the school, and the charter reform movement have flourished since.

The next chapter (chapter 4) follows up on Chan and Vaughn Next Century Learning Center since 2004. She shares in her remarkable stories that it was her devotion and perseverance stemming from her own beginnings as an immigrant that fueled her desire to offer a better life for all of her students. This devotion, perseverance, and belief in the American public school system as a means for improvement in life drove her success for her school and within the new charter school landscape.

Chan spent endless hours learning to navigate the early years of the charter school movement despite an initially contentious relationship with the district. She built a strong, creative team to convert the struggling school. She even mortgaged her home to keep the school afloat while awaiting government funding to come through. Today she is a national voice for social reform in education, and the Vaughn Next Century Learning Center can be viewed as a model learning community.

Chan is not the only leader who was prepared to sacrifice personal funds and lifestyle for the cause of her community. She exemplifies the unwavering dedication we found in all of our leaders; two more from the original book and six others added that we discovered had converted to charter status when researching schools for *Journeys*.

Story after story tells of leaders who were and continue to be devoted to a vision. Each leader's mission may be different, whether it is providing an arts-based curriculum or a classical education or project-based learning. However, each leader shares a common focus to provide a high-quality educational experience for their students, even, as so many of them found, if this involved much deeper involvement in their communities and even wider policy change. Whether each leader set his or her needs aside, or those needs became completely overshadowed or replaced by their mission to improve a school, they all dove into efforts building entire communities focused on a foundation of helping the children of their community.

Numerous interviews, dialogues, investigations, and observations have resulted in these three books about charter schools and their leaders. We have learned much, but much of it boils down a simple fact. These successful charter school leaders all possess an unwavering commitment to their school communities, and every one of them sees problems as opportunities.

They also all embody strong relationship-building skills and are able to construct teams that not only share the same passion but are skilled in the essential areas needed to run a publicly accountable yet independent educational entity, the charter school, and are ready and willing to wield leverage where needed and possible. Their journeys reflect challenges that may drive others to seek opportunities elsewhere, but to them, were well worth their passion and the dedication of their lives to their communities over time.

We believe that our adventures in meeting and learning about the journeys of so many successful charter school leaders across our country have made us better leaders; however, it is our mission to share that knowledge with others to more widely impact the improvement of education through educational leadership. These stories chronicle the improved educational opportunities that can become available to communities, particularly to the under-represented, when cumbersome regulations are loosened while accountability and high-quality standards are met under the guidance of committed leaders.

We are grateful that these individual leaders shared their heartfelt journeys with us, and we hope that their lessons in devotion, perseverance, humility, learning, and love are reflected in the pages of our books. While the visions were different for each leader, passion and dedication have been the same. Successfully changing to charter is more than just "buy-in." It's a way of life.

Part I

NUTS AND BOLTS OF CHANGING TO CHARTER

Chapter 1

Charter Schools Defined

"Charter schools" have existed for nearly thirty years in the United States; however, misinformation abounds. Some of this misinformation is channeled through those studying public K–12 education. These scholars and students often miss important factors that would contribute to a full and more accurate understanding of charter schools. The misrepresentations may be traced back to some difficult battles that have occurred within the education setting, and parties on both sides of the charter school debate have assumed poor intent and played loose with the facts.

In a sense, time may heal wounds, but, in some areas, the scars remain. Regrettably, one of those scars is a lack of understanding that cuts across many circles of influence—political, legal, familial, educational, and social. For instance, some people thought that charter schools were for-profit organizations or were just another type of magnet school. Still, other groups believed that charter schools were "private" schools that received public funding.

According to the National Charter School Resource Center (NCSRC), an organization sponsored by the U.S. Department of Education, charter schools are defined as "independently managed, publicly funded schools operating under a 'charter' or a contract between the school and the state of jurisdiction, allowing for significant autonomy and flexibility."[1]

Charter schools themselves contribute to this confusion as the sector is complicated with differences abounding between charter school types. As charter schools are state regulated based upon individual state laws, adopted regulations, or proffered policies, we cannot generalize to the granular details but must stay focused on the state level. If one were to seek specifics for a particular state, an important first piece of advice would be to research that state's laws, regulations, policies, and procedures. We can, however, clarify some basic terminology that establishes a frame upon which a true understanding of the charter model can be constructed. The terms "publicly funded" and "charter" are significant in the definition cited above. To have a clear understanding of charter schools both terms must be understood and applied correctly.

PUBLICLY FUNDED

Charter schools are "publicly funded," meaning that state funds, and in some cases federal funds, are allotted to the schools for the purpose of educating students. Pending the structure of a charter school in accordance with state law, some charters can receive federal funds such as special education or Title I funds. As a condition upon accepting these monies, charter schools must assure compliance with both the state and federal funding requirements, including all testing requirements, like traditional public schools.

Charter school funding is determined by state laws and regulations, but whether or not a charter school ever opens its doors is totally dependent upon the number of students choosing to attend. Some states call this average daily attendance (ADA) while others refer to it as average daily membership (ADM). Charter schools, as a nonprofit, may also apply for private, competitive grants.

THE CHARTER

"Charter" is another key term in the definition of charter schools. The charter is an agreement or a contract between the governing board of the school and the entity that decided to grant the charter—an authorizing entity. Charter authorizing entities can include state boards of education, institutions of higher learning, school districts, or other nonprofit entities. Again, process details are state-specific; yet, these authorizers are granted authority by law to create an application cycle that includes a call for proposals, application submission, review, awarding a charter, and renewal procedures.

A charter document describes the required components of the school such as mission and vision, instructional program, governance structure, personnel plan, budgetary assumptions, enrollment projections, and academic accountability measures. The charter often incorporates the application to set the stipulations for how the school will perform and be measured over the duration of its lifetime. Any amendments to the charter must be approved, in advance, by the authorizing entity to ensure fidelity to the school's operational aspects.

Charter schools exist because of a dual exchange—more operational freedom alongside more outcome accountability. Although free from some requirements (e.g., teacher certification), charter schools do face increased accountability measures in that they can be closed for poor performance whether in finances, academics, or operations. Charter schools cannot discriminate in admission policies. Charter schools cannot charge tuition for students. Charter schools cannot pick and choose student enrollments as they are required to utilize a lottery if more students apply than seats are available. Charter schools cannot ignore performance on state-mandated assessments. Charter schools cannot spend public dollars any way they want because they are bound by state and federal mandates.

While charter schools may look very different, they all must adhere to regulations and policies much like traditional public schools. The volunteer governing board is legally responsible for every aspect of school operation, and authorizers are expected to regularly monitor the school's outcomes. As part of their monitoring responsibilities, authorizers may conduct site visits, hold desk audits, perform document reviews (e.g., board meeting minutes), examine financial records, or host informal conversations. These monitoring protocols vary across authorizing organizations, but their intent is the same—judge the charter school's outcomes to forge a determination in whether to renew or terminate a charter.

We, as authors, have studied vastly different schools from project-based, arts-based schools to direct-instruction schools to classical schools, and these pedagogical variances highlight their operational freedom. While each school held true to its mission and vision, they did so while successfully meeting their state's required accountability measures, thus showcasing their outcome focus. Simply put, a failure in either area would compel an authorizer to review programmatic adherence and performance achievement to determine the future status of that charter school.

FOR-PROFIT OR NONPROFIT

One of the most popular questions involving charter schools is whether they are not-for-profit or for-profit entities. Charter schools, in accordance with state laws, operate as a public school, and the volunteer governing board is a nonprofit entity. As such, charter schools are not-for-profit organizations. These governing boards are constituted in accordance with their Articles of Corporation and Bylaws which vary widely but must comply with state mandates. The Articles and Bylaws describe the number and term of board members, procedures for electing new members, committee/meeting structure, and basic parliamentary procedures. These documents, along with the charter, determine how the board will, much like their traditional counterparts, partner with for-profit companies to deliver services for students.

Without question, the majority of charter schools are governed by volunteer charter school boards but all of them partner with other for-profit businesses to assist them in their school operation, just like traditional schools and districts. The discussion of profit in education is often segmented only for the charter school sector; however, the issue is broader than most people will permit the discussion to go. For instance, simply answer this question: do textbook organizations, athletic companies, furniture businesses, construction firms, or insurance corporations make profit by working with traditional schools? The answer is an unequivocal yes.

This question turns, however, in the role of what is called an educational management organization (EMO). These entities provide an array of services and expertise to the governing boards in exchange for a fee. The services, just to name a few, could include marketing, curriculum, financial bookkeeping, professional development, and facility acquisition. How widespread is the presence of EMOs within the charter community? According to the National Alliance of Public Charter Schools (NAPCS), less than 15 percent of charter schools are managed by a for-profit EMO.[2] Despite the small footprint, some states are now taking steps to put forward specific regulations surrounding the for-profit status of charter schools.

During the 2017–18 legislative session, California included language in the law that "a charter renewal or material revision application shall not operate as, or be operated by, a for-profit corporation." The legislation goes further by defining the terms "operate as, or be operated by," to include the following factors: providing services before the board has approved in a public meeting, making budgetary expenditures not approved by the board, employing/dismissing employees of the school, and controlling membership of the board.[3]

CHARTER SCHOOL TYPES

While we are focusing on leaders of conversion charter schools, it is only one of many types of charters; and as mentioned above, the different forms often contribute to additional confusion. The most prevalent charter school iterations include the following: Independent, Charter Management Organizations (CMO), Vender Operated Schools (VOS), and Hybrid Charter Schools and Conversion Charter Schools. Each of these public charter schools is bound by their Charter Agreements to follow the same state and federal regulations while offering enrollment to all students. These schools do, however, fluctuate in their form of management.

Independent Charter Schools are the most common making up two-thirds of all charter schools across the country.[4] This familiar type of nonprofit charter school is independently overseen by a volunteer governing board. Independent charter schools stand alone and bear total responsibility for operating the charter school. While there may be several schools (K–5, 6–8, and 9–12), the charter school as a whole is led by one governing board through their administrative and staffing hires. This school is not a part of a larger organization but may contract out certain services to entities that have found profitability in a niche market.

The most commonly contracted out services are interrelated—management of student information services and the financial operation. If these contractors make mistakes that result in an authorizer investigation, the governing board remains the responsible party to answer questions or suffer consequences. Ultimately, the authorizer expects this board to vet contractors carefully and to monitor their work regularly.

CMOs are a little more complicated to define as their definition varies greatly due to their organizational construct. Where the definitions converse with unity in terms of organizational control as well as a number of separate charter schools, historically, a CMO holds the charter that has been granted by the authorizer and operates at least three separate schools.

These separate schools need a little further clarification because models differ—the schools could be exact duplicates of grade span and mission (e.g., three K–8 schools that offer classical education), continuation of grade span but divided into separate buildings with separate school numbers for accountability purposes (e.g., one K–5, one 6–8, and one 9–12 school), or a mixture of anything else (e.g., one K–5 arts-focused school, one 9–12 career-ready high school, and one K–12 direct-instruction school). The models depend upon the individual state laws, the capacity of the CMO, and the approval of the authorizer.

Despite the model differences, the CMO controls all school operations, including instructional practices, personnel policies, finances, and operations. CMOs can be nonprofit or for-profit entities, depending upon what state policy will permit to occur.

Often confused with CMOs are schools that fall into the VOS category. VOS entities are contracted, by local charter school boards, to provide a myriad of services to more than three separate schools; however, unlike a CMO, they do not hold the charter from the authorizer. The key, here, is contracted work with more than one school or it would simply be an Independent Charter School.

The VOS services range widely from a singular offering (e.g., professional development for teachers) to the school's entire operations (e.g., compliance, academics, finances, facilities). The most distinguishing factor between a

CMO and VOS is in that possession of the charter. Since the VOS does not hold the charter, they report directly and regularly to the volunteer governing board. The VOS, much like the CMO, can be nonprofit or for-profit organizations based upon state law.

Hybrid Charter Schools are an iteration within the charter space in that they include characteristics of both CMOs and VOSs. As the name implies, Hybrid Charter Schools may include a CMO that holds the charter but contracts services from a VOS or multiple VOSs. Again, these Hybrid organizations may be for-profit or nonprofit. According to research conducted in 2017, only 1 percent of charter school organizations are in this category.[5]

CONVERSION CHARTER SCHOOLS

According to the NAPCS, Conversion Charter Schools, the topic of this book, are charter schools authorized by the state or local school district to take over an existing traditional public school often as a result of issues with school quality or poor growth. In other instances that do not include lackluster performance, an existing public school and/or private school could petition an authorizer authority to convert to charter status. The motivations for this self-selected conversion vary and will be discussed in-depth below.

Most states (thirty-nine of the forty-four) with existing charter school laws permit conversions according to the Education Commission of the States (ECS).[6] For whatever reason determined by their legislatures, Arizona, Nevada, New Mexico, and Washington do not allow for conversions. It is also important to note that while thirty-nine states allow for conversions, each state has its own stipulations and regulations regarding conversion charter schools. As an example, Texas law grants the district an opportunity to charter status creating what is called "a home-rule school district charter," but that conversion would require a majority vote in an election where "at least 25 percent of a school district's registered votes participate."[7] As you can image, this mandate acts as a considerable hurdle that is yet to be overcome.

The largest percentage of conversion charter schools is located in the following states: California, Iowa, Maryland, Georgia, Arkansas, and Louisiana. While the primary focus of this book is California, we will include case studies from the Carolinas as well. With the legislatively imposed cap in North Carolina having been lifted nearly a decade ago, that state has seen an increase in its number of conversion schools—particularly the private to charter variety.

Conversion charter schools can be led by the district or managed independently or by a CMO. Three of the conversions detailed in this book include both types, but they are all nonprofit charter schools. Their stories highlight benefits of converting failing traditional schools and founders focused on the ability to tailor instruction/curriculum to better meet the needs of the population and budgeting. With charter school autonomy, curriculum can be based on the mission and vision of the newly formed charter with monies allocated to provide the professional development needed to match those needs. Freedom from bureaucratic regulations allows energy to be directed at the charter school level; and if that focus needs to change, it can do so quickly for programmatic improvement.

These conversion charter schools were converted from traditional public schools in the early 1990s: they are Vaughn Next Century Learning Center, Fenton Center Public Charter School, and Feaster-Edison Charter School. Each conversion school has matured in the past twenty-five years modifying their names and organizational structures; however, each original leader continues to serve a role in the conversion charter school's existence. More can be learned about the schools and their leadership journeys through specific case studies in the book.

Shifting from this theoretical explanation of a charter school conversion, this book examines motivations for conversion by highlighting real-world examples. This book includes application expectations and what authorizers consider in their review of charter proposals. Ultimately, the intent of this book is to inform.

NOTES

1. National Charter School Resource Center, "What Is a Charter School?" accessed December 31, 2018, from https://charterschoolcenter.ed.gov/what-is-a-charter-school.

2. National Alliance for Public Charter Schools, "Charter Schools FAQ" accessed December 31, 2018, from https://www.publiccharters.org/about-charter-schools/charter-school-faq.

3. California Legislative Information, "Bill No. 406, Approved by Governor September 7, 2018" accessed September 29, 2019, from https://leginfo.legislature.ca.gov/faces/billTextClient.xhtml?bill_id=201720180AB406.

4. James L. Woodworth, Margaret E. Raymond, Chunping Han, Yohannes Negassi, W. Payton Richardson, and Will Snow, *Charter management organizations 2017*, (Stanford, CA: CREDO – Center for Research on Education Outcomes), 1.

5. Ibid, 3.

6. Education Commission of the States, "50-State Comparison" accessed January 19, 2019, from http://ecs.force.com/mbdata/mbquestNB2C?rep=CS1702.

7. Texas Education Code, "TEC §§12.021-12.022" accessed on October 6, 2019, from https://statutes.capitol.texas.gov/Docs/ED/htm/ED.12.htm.

Chapter 2

Why Change to Charter?

Chapter 1 discusses the conversion model at the definition level; this chapter digs deeper into the philosophical level with one very important word—why. Excluding charters that were forcibly converted due to poor academic performance, why would an existing public or private school pursue this pathway? What, about this model, is so appealing that school officials would give up their known history to move into a different space that exerts so much pressure for performance?

The private school conversion motivations are a little more understandable—the allure of public funding. Private schools traditionally operate from a tuition-based model, with fundraising as a supplement; thus, converting to a public school shifts that model to a per-student allocation. In theory, public funding makes the budget easier to balance and opens the school to a wider student population. Instead of relying upon only families that can afford the tuition, these newly converted charters are open to any child eligible to attend a public school.

This draw of public funding becomes even more appealing during times of economic downturn as fewer families are eligible to afford the private school tuition. In fact, a North Carolina Charter applicant referenced this issue back in 2013. With its enrollment dipping from 436 students to 361, the private school faced a six-digit loss of funding. Note this specific passage from the application:

> The decline in the local economy has taken its toll on Vance County. Incomes have decreased significantly since 2008. 2009–2011 represented some of the darkest economic times for Vance County in several decades. This has not left Kerr-Vance Academy untouched with regard to economic performance. The depressed economy, in conjunction with the opening of two new charter

schools have made for challenging financial times for KVA. Given the choice of a tuition-free, high quality academic program at a charter school versus a tuition-based, high quality academic program at a private school, many families have found themselves forgoing the latter in favor of the former. KVA has seen a decline in enrollment from 2010 to present due to a significant increase in parents unable to pay tuition.[1]

Needless to say, the private-to-public metamorphosis is a dream scenario if the law permits the conversation and if the proposal receives approval from the authorizing authority. Within that promising situation, however, major pitfalls exist that must be overcome.

CONVERTING A PRIVATE SCHOOL

Without a doubt, the conversion process becomes more challenging for private schools. Yes, they possess history, facilities, and current students, but those aspects create issues for the possible charter school. The private school's history or school culture may have to undergo serious modification to convert to charter status forcing them to use a valuation model to gauge opportunity costs of loss in the current against the gain in the future.

For instance, the school may have previously required all students to wear uniforms that were purchased by the families; however, this expectation would be a barrier to enrollment for families that could not afford the uniform purchase. As such, a school undergoing the conversion process would have to decide what to do about school uniforms—keep the policy but offer assistance to families or scrap the policy entirely. This issue merely scratches the surface; but a deeper, historical matter can cause an immediate identity crisis for the school.

As an existing private school, the school leaders discussed, pondered, drafted, adopted, and lived one mission statement. In doing so, the school planned its instructional and operational plans based upon that specific mission which, sometimes, has to be completely overhauled for conversion to work. In September 2016, the Mountain Island Day School charter application was filed with the NC Office of Charter Schools. This application sought to convert an existing private, Christian school that featured "blessing before meals, an opening prayer each day, weekly Bible classes and chapel."[2]

With the North Carolina educational code—§ 115C-218.50—stating that a charter school "shall be nonsectarian in its programs,"[3] Mountain Island Day School had to sacrifice its mission, curriculum, operating procedures, and expectations for students. This decision may have been the first-ever in

North Carolina, and the founders understood these changes could repel long-standing families and supporters of the school.

FACILITIES

Despite receiving unanimous approval, the hard work was just beginning. The founders of Mountain Island Day School then took steps to immediately address religious issues on the website and facility to ensure proper separation of church and state. The prior building was known for its steeple and large cross, but modifications were necessary to comply with legal requirements.[4] These facility modifications, revisions to the website, and other responsibilities (e.g., marketing their school) had to be addressed without public funding as part of the process to become a charter school.

Facilities also create ownership, liability, and financial issues. The organization entity that owned the property being utilized by the private school controls those capital assets and must decide on next steps. In some instances, the prior landlord will simply lease those facilities to the newly converted charter school to prevent a spatial vacancy or to cover previously incurred financial liabilities. In a North Carolina conversion application, the prior landlord did "not intend to transfer its assets or its liabilities" to the new charter school but would, instead, "provide for an operating lease on the assets" to then "use lease revenues to service existing debt."[5]

In other instances, the property is outright sold or gifted to a nonprofit entity. One private school conversion in North Carolina did an interesting split of assets—the "real property" was sold to a family trust and the deed would transfer upon final payment while "all contents" of the facility remained the property of the newly formed charter school and would convey upon its approval.[6] Neither of the situations mentioned above is wrong, but some additional questions by the authorizer assuredly arose from the dealings to ensure the budgets were fiscally sound. The specifics of facility arrangements are additional considerations that any private school conversion will face and have to explain to stakeholders and authorizing entities as the process moves forward.

STUDENT ENROLLMENT

Private schools also face a specific challenge due to their previous existence and a current student body. The choice to convert from private to public means that the school must hold an open enrollment period, whereby, they determine if they must hold a lottery for students. For example, if the school has 450 seats and more than 600 applications for those seats, then a blind lottery is held to determine the school's enrollment. Students previously enrolled in the private school cannot be given an advantage over any new applicants, and this stark realization can create parental opposition toward the conversion effort. The newly converted public school must act in such a way that its integrity is without question as many will be watching and scrutinizing every decision regarding enrollment.

In August 2013, a new North Carolina private school conversion had to reopen its enrollment due to a complaint filed with the NC Department of Public Instruction. The conversion school increased its grade level caps from kindergarten through eighth grade beyond those approved by the state, meaning that they would not receive funding for those additional students. The allegation rested upon the fact that families not affiliated with the private school were not given the same opportunity at enrollment as were the previously enrolled private school students. While the school denied that any families were not given the fair opportunity, they did recognize how their actions could have been perceived as unethical.[7]

The heart of the matter focused on whether or not proper notice and time for enrollment were given to families not affiliated with the private school. In fact, the complaint letter provided information indicating confusion within the enrollment process—multiple days of enrollment leading to multiple days of possible lottery, only one day's notice of accepting applications, a short time-frame to complete enrollment documents, and applications would only be accepted during the school day.[8]

While school officials denied any wrongdoing and presented a plan to try and rectify the situation, the motivations and intentions of the school were called into question. Any private school converting to charter status must take seriously their efforts to host an unimpeachable enrollment process and lottery.

CONVERTING A PUBLIC SCHOOL

Conversely, converting an existing public school to a charter school has its own unique aspects too. To gain a better understanding of the differences, the focus here is on a specific example from South Carolina in 2006—the Orange Grove Elementary School became the Orange Grove Charter School. One needs to understand the policy and authorizer environment to create a foundation for why the school took specific actions in order to convert to charter status. Whereas this is one policy environment for public school conversion, understand that each state will have laws that govern conversion status that readers, if pondering a conversion, will need to know and understand during the application process.

APPLICATION PROCESS

Every state has its own application and process to determine which proposals will receive a charter. A cursory look across the applications themselves reflect the uniqueness and variety within charter school laws. As stated previously, NAPCS does not go deep in the charter conversion area by merely recommending the inclusion of a stakeholder approval section to the regular charter application. Each authorizer, pending their state's law, can go deeper with questioning; and some, due to their local context, have done just that.

North Carolina created an entire section to address conversions of charter schools because the advisory board that reviewed these proposals believed more information was needed. After an applicant selects their designation as a conversation proposal, the application divides between public and private school conversion. A public school conversion is much simpler within the application as candidates must provide this information: the six-digit school identification number and evidences of support for the conversion. The evidences sought by the authorizer "must include:

1. Statement of Support signed by the majority of the teachers and instructional support personnel currently employed at the school,
2. Last payroll outlining current staff receiving compensation from the traditional public school,
3. Current school enrollment, and
4. Parental support of the conversion."[9]

Later in the application, questions arise on student lottery as any converted public school must give preference to students who lived in the attendance zone previously served.

For private school conversion applicants, their level of scrutiny increases significantly with more robust questioning. First, the previously existing private school's name and location must be provided. Second, the application demands the compilation of a three-year financial history, including any IRS-900 forms, to review the financial viability of the private school.

Undoubtedly, this request seeks to gauge the acumen of the business leaders and if the real conversion motive was to cover previously accrued debt. Finally, the application digs deep with questions covering these topics: rationale for conversion, compliance with nonsectarian clause of the law, enrollment/demographic trends of the last three years, evidence of the private school's academic success, and staffing plans (including possible turnover due to the state's teacher certification requirements).[10]

AUTHORIZER CONSIDERATIONS

Once the application has been packaged and sent to the authorizer, the applicant wait begins. As these charter proposals can be more than 150 pages, and many proposals are submitted each cycle, the review process takes time. Authorizing entities often read and score an application determining which should come forward to receive a face-to-face interview. The applicants discover the concerns of that initial review and then prepare to address them in a formal interview. When the review and interview are completed, the authorizing entity votes on whether or not to extend the charter.

The process for conversion charters operates just like others; however, the depth of questioning faced by these applicants can get much deeper. For example, the chair of the NC Charter School Advisory Board (CSAB), in reviewing a charter school conversion proposal, did not mince his words when he said, "I feel like there's another layer of scrutiny that should be applied." One of his colleagues focused upon private school conversions by indicating their board would judge a candidate's gravity in commitment to become a public school and watching for any attempt of transferring private debt to the public coffers.[11] Authorizer board members want to see schools succeed and must ask diligent questions in order to make the difficult decisions.

BACK-TO-BACK APPLICATIONS IN ONE MEETING

At its regularly scheduled meeting in December 2017, the NC Charter School Advisory Board experienced a rather interesting situation—back-to-back private school conversions in a formal interview. The applicants were about as different as possible: Hobgood Academy resided in the rural, eastern part of the state, served grades K–12, and would close unless the conversion gained approval. Conversely, Mountain Island resided in the suburban, western part of the state and was religiously based.

Hobgood Academy, where no prior charter school existed, received a vigorous debate. Concerns were voiced, but members of the board were sensitive to the fact that no public school choice existed in the area. Ultimately, this application was denied in a split vote due to concerns about debt transfer and the grade structure of the school. While officials representing the proposal could not effectively answer the questions posed by the review board, they were reminded that they could "apply in the following year as long as the applicant fixes the issues."[12]

This applicant did return in the next cycle and went through the process again. To address many of their concerns, they partnered with a CMO for limited services—financials and student data—while completely overhauling their board. Further, the school modified its grade configuration to focus on K–8 leaving 9–12 as private. This change garnered quite a few questions to ensure the two entities were separated in every matter so as not to cause an audit finding.

Board members were better prepared and answered questions to the satisfaction of the authorizer. In fact, the authorizing entity thanked them for their "hard work and dedication" while stating they are "now ready for conversion." Prior to the vote, the authorizing board chair said the following: "This is a strong application and an indication of the importance of a rigorous application process."[13] Knowing that they received unanimous approval reveals an important lesson—a negative vote does not end all hope for an application in the future.

Mountain Island, while receiving unanimous approval, faced its own challenges during the interview. Concern arose around the name of the school as it resembled the name of another charter school in that same area. Discussion also hovered around the topic of debt and note to the words of a CSAB member, "the school must figure out the financials" but they did "not see the same glaring financial issues from the prior school."

As a motion was made to approve the proposal, an objection arose causing that motion to be withdrawn. A member noticed a particular course requirement that could exclude students and they were not "comfortable recommending approval of another charter with that piece."[14] The issue was resolved, but it reveals the detailed analysis and review that all charter applicants must face—whether they succeed or fail in their endeavor to earn a charter from their state authorizers.

STAKEHOLDER SUPPORT EXPECTATION

NAPCS, in publishing its model charter school law, has defined conversion charters and included information recommended for inclusion in state charter school laws. Within the expectations for a charter application, NAPCS includes this singular endorsement for the law:

> In the case of a proposed charter public school that plans to convert an existing non-charter public school to charter public school status, the application shall additionally require the applicants to demonstrate support for the proposed charter public school conversion by a petition signed by a majority of the teachers, a petition signed by a majority of parents of students in the existing non-charter public school, or a portion signed by a majority of the school. Board.[15]

Notice the use of the term "or" in the groups that should be petitioned for approval, meaning that only one should be set as an expectation. The intent is without question—ensuring that stakeholders have an opportunity to voice their opinions regarding the possible conversion—because NAPCS understands the unforeseen and often unstated issues that can arise before, during, and after the conversion process.

South Carolina, rather than inserting language into their charter law, promulgated regulations that set forth the expectations for public school conversion; and the State Board of Education went further than NAPCS recommended by instituting at least two venues of support: parental and staff. Evidence, within the charter application, shall include that an "adequate number of parents or legal guardians with students eligible to attend the proposed school" support it, meaning the proposed budget is solid.

While this requirement exists for all charter schools, conversion charters had to go one step further in that two-thirds "of the voting parents or legal guardians voted to support" filing of the conversion application. The regulation removes all doubt of how this process should work by dictating that "parents or guardians shall have one vote for each of their children enrolled in the school."[16] The law recognizes that not all parents want to offer their opinion but emphasizes that each parent should be given the opportunity to voice those concerns.

In turning to the staff, South Carolina breaks from NAPCS by adding instructional staff to the mix of school-based officials that must be solicited for approval. The broader group of school staff serves as an insurance policy that protects the students. If the majority of the staff is committed to the conversion, then they would, most likely, continue working at the school after the process concluded. This stability protected school culture and offered some familiarity as the winds of change were about to gust.

South Carolina also added an interesting twist to the conversion process that certainly helped with the staff vote but potentially created future budgetary issues. The regulation specifically says that those working at the school before conversion that chose to stay "will remain employees of the local school district with the same compensation and benefits including any future increases."[17] Teachers, who may have been undecided on the actual conversion and worried about compensation or benefits, were granted immediate and future relief.

The school had to create a budget that covered any future increase for these individuals as the district may offer salary or benefit incentives. The larger budget implication faced by school administrators hinged upon the hiring of new teachers who would not be members of the local school district. This could possibly create a dual-salary system within the building that would erode school culture; yet, astute administrators address that issue on the front end to prevent its occurrence.

Once the recommendations have been made and voting has been finalized, the real work for the successful applicants begins; and the duration of that work can depend upon state law and authorizing entities. Some states—both

North and South Carolina—require charter applicants to go through a mandatory year of planning. This rationale was rooted in historical figures reflecting earlier struggles of these schools.

For example, earlier approved charters granted in March for an opening less than six months away became viewed as unrealistic with such a short turnaround. Over time, policymakers recognized that not all applicants need that mandatory year and created a process to fast track those applicants. In the case of North Carolina conversion schools, most received motions for "accelerated opening," and that decision makes sense.[18] With already existing facilities, name recognition, students, and faculty, the plausibility of those schools opening quickly is higher than an applicant lacking those aspects.

As shown, attention to the detail of the ever-changing state charter statutes is critical for accessing the most up-to-date requirements and resources. One national resource is the Education Commission of the States (ECS), which was founded in 1967 to share information, tools, and competence across all the states. While the ECS provides basic information on charter schools, the greatest value is their compilation of in-depth "individual state profiles." These state-specific profiles cover nearly every area imaginable—accountability measures, school finance, teacher status—and includes statutory citations.[19]

The statutory details from South Carolina's conversion process are important to understand the story of Orange Grove Elementary School in chapter 9. At the time of Orange Grove's conversion, it was only the second school in South Carolina to go through that process—ironically within the same district. As the reader can surmise, part II will shift considerably from theory to practice by presenting actual case studies of schools that have successfully converted to charter status. These individual examples cover a cross-section of the country—from California to the Carolinas—and highlight critical leaders, historical steps, and situational distinctives in the quest for individual autonomy within the charter sector. Their stories offer direction and resources for anyone currently considering the conversion process.

NOTES

1. Kerr-Vance Charter Application, pp. 37–38, accessed on October 6, 2019 from http://www.ncpublicschools.org/docs/charterschools/applications/15-16/kerrvance.pdf.

2. Ann Doss Helms, "Christianity is Out, Public Money is in as Charlotte School Makes Rare Conversion," accessed on October 5, 2019 from https://www.charlotteobserver.com/news/local/education/article197550394.html.

3. NC Education Code, Article 14A, Section 115C, accessed on October 15, 2019 from https://www.ncleg.net/EnactedLegislation/Statutes/PDF/ByArticle/Chapter_115c/Article_14A.pdf.

4. Helms, Christianity Is Out.
5. Kerr-Vance Charter Application, p. 38.
6. Hobgood Academy Charter School Application, p. 36, accessed on September 28, 2019 from http://www.ncpublicschools.org/docs/charterschools/applications/20-21/hobgood.pdf.
7. Ali Rockett, "Robeson County's Southeastern Academy Reopening Enrollment, Adding more Students," accessed on October 6, 2019 from https://www.fayobserver.com/article/20130807/News/308079792.
8. Social Coalition for Social Justice complaint letter to the NC Office of Charter Schools, accessed on October 5, 2019 from http://pulse.ncpolicywatch.org/wp-content/uploads/2013/08/Southeastern-Academy-Complaint.pdf.
9. NC Charter School Application, p. 11 and 23, accessed October 13, 2019 from http://www.ncpublicschools.org/charterschools/applications accessed.
10. Ibid., pp. 11–12.
11. Helms, Christianity is Out.
12. "Minutes of the NC Charter School Advisory Board Meeting on December 17, 2017," p. 12, accessed on October 19, 2019 at http://www.ncpublicschools.org/docs/charterschools/board/minutes12-2017.pdf.
13. "Minutes of the NC Charter School Advisory Board Meeting on January 14, 2019," pp. 24–25, accessed on October 20, 2019 at http://www.ncpublicschools.org/docs/charterschools/board/minutes01-2019.pdf.
14. Ibid., p. 12 and 13.
15. National Alliance for Public Charter Schools, "Model Charter School Law," p. 58, accessed October 5, 2019 from https://www.publiccharters.org/about-charter-schools/charter-school-faq.
16. SC State Board of Education Regulation R 43-601, "Procedures and Standards for Review Charter School Applications," p. 2, accessed on October 5, 2019 from https://ed.sc.gov/scdoe/assets/File/stateboard/documents/601.pdf.
17. Ibid., p. 1.
18. NC Charter School Advisory Board Meeting Minutes (December 2017), p. 12.
19. The Education Commission of the States charter school state profiles can be located here: https://www.ecs.org/charter-schools-policies-state-profiles.

Part II

JOURNEYS OF ADVENTUROUS LEADERS

Chapter 3

New Kids on the Block

Vaughn Next Century Learning Center, 2004

By Yvonne Chan

Under the leadership of Dr. Yvonne Chan, Vaughn Street Elementary School in Los Angeles became Vaughn Next Century Learning Center, the nation's first independent, urban, conversion charter school. Chan and Vaughn Next Century have gone on to push the idea of school reform to its limit, creating inspired solutions to many endemic urban school problems. She has led a transformation that has seen dramatic increases in student achievement and attendance, a sharp reduction in crime, and the creation of the Family Center to provide for the needs of the school's primarily low-income, minority families.

Additionally, Chan has been instrumental in mustering the support and resources needed to expand the school from its original elementary grades to a pre-K–12 learning center. Vaughn families have become involved in their students' education as well as in the larger community, thanks to the efforts of Chan and the Vaughn staff. Vaughn was named a California Distinguished School in 1995, a National Blue Ribbon School by the U.S. Department of Education in 1996. It has been visited by Hillary Clinton, U.S. legislators, and dignitaries from around the world. Chan, who immigrated alone to the United States from Hong Kong at the age of seventeen, has worked since 1968 in various regular education, special education, and administrative capacities within the Los Angeles Unified School District.

On March 6, 1999, seventeen-year old Francisco was shot to death in front of his home, apparently the victim of gang rivalry; he was a block away from his elementary school. His younger brother Eddie, a fourth-grader at the school, now named Vaughn Next Century Learning Center, is a member of the student council and is determined to go to college. The brothers led a different life because their school offered them different types of opportunities.

Vaughn is a neighborhood public school located in Pacoima, a designated "Empowerment Zone" in the city of Los Angeles, due to its extreme poverty and high-crime status. Since 1951, Vaughn Street Elementary was cited as one of the worst schools in the Los Angeles Unified School District. Single-digit test scores and poor attendance were a pattern. It served 1,050 K–6 students: 94.9 percent Hispanic, 5 percent African American, 0.1 percent Asian; 80.5 percent were Spanish-speaking English learners; 97.4 percent received free or reduced-price lunch.

"Francisco was shot to death in front of his home . . .; he was a block from his elementary school."

Francisco attended Vaughn beginning in kindergarten. He was always in classrooms with thirty-two to thirty-five students. The school provided 163 instructional days on a 3-track schedule due to overcrowding. Francisco was bused briefly to another school in 1991 for four months because of a court-ordered desegregation plan. Francisco had special needs that were not identified until grade three.

Vaughn had a psychologist only one day per week; counseling and after-school tutoring were not available. As soon as he was identified as a severely learning-disabled student, he was bused to another district school for special education services. Vaughn did not offer a special day-class program, due to lack of classroom space and personnel. In order for Francisco to return to Vaughn, his neighborhood school, his parents had to waive the right to intensive special education services beginning in grade four. Chronic asthma prevented him from maintaining regular attendance. He did not qualify for public health care, and Vaughn had a school nurse only one day per week.

During Francisco's entire education at Vaughn, he was taught by only one fully credentialed teacher. All his other teachers were on emergency permits. Vaughn was a "hard-to-staff" inner-city school. Each year, the school lost 30 percent of its thirty-nine teachers. Every week, Francisco's classroom was vandalized. New computers were stolen before they were unpacked. Student suspension rose to 12 percent, and fights between Hispanic and African American students occurred daily. When Francisco was transferred to the neighborhood middle school, he had not passed the bilingual redesignation test and was still reading in Spanish with limited skills in English.

Vaughn converted to an independent charter school in 1993. Francisco's brother Eddie started at Vaughn Next Century Learning Center at the age of three in 1994. Prior to entering kindergarten, Eddie had two years of preschool education at Vaughn, which provides space to the sponsoring district and the Los Angeles County Office of Education to operate the State Preschool and the Federal Head Start programs. The class size at Vaughn is kept at twenty students in all grades. An extended school year provides Eddie with a full 200 days of instruction as well as daily after-school academic and enrichment activities until 6:00 p.m. Overcrowding is no longer a problem; Vaughn has eliminated the multitrack schedule by building an additional fifty-six classrooms since the charter school conversion.

> **"Vaughn, which failed Francisco miserably, provides Eddie with a world-class education. . . . The student demographics have not changed, but the adults at Vaughn have."**

Though Eddie was also identified as a learning-disabled student, he received intervention as early as kindergarten. Services are provided in an inclusive setting that includes co-teaching by general and special education teachers, speech therapy, peer tutoring, after-school tutoring, family counseling, and attendance and motivation activities. Eddie successfully exited from the special education program in grade three. When Eddie has health-care needs, Vaughn's site-based clinic operated by the Los Angeles County Health Department provides immunization, medication, medical tests, and various primary care services.

Along with his friends, Eddie enjoys surfing the internet during class to conduct research, write reports, and email overseas pen pals in China. Eddie's mother takes a GED class at Vaughn offered by the district Adult Education Division. Her classroom is right next door to Eddie's. She usually waves to her son after her class. On her way to the Vaughn Family Center, where she volunteers child care services, she keeps an eye on the new construction site. She knows that Eddie, after completing grade five at Vaughn, will continue his middle school and high school education at this Little School That Could.

Vaughn, which failed Francisco miserably, provided Eddie with a world-class education. Vaughn Next Century Learning Center is located at the same site, serving 1,300 students from special education infants to grade five: 95.3 percent Hispanic, 4.6 percent African American, 0.1 percent Asian; 76.5 percent are Spanish-speaking English learners; 97.6 percent receive free or reduced-price lunch. The student demographics have not changed, but the adults at Vaughn have.

OUT OF THE BOX: WE COULD DO NO WORSE

Vaughn Street Elementary was a typical large, urban public school impacted by multiple social stresses. I was assigned to Vaughn in May 1990 amid twenty-four teacher grievances, two lawsuits, ongoing intergroup disputes, and three death threats directed toward the principal. Vaughn was the third public school where I assumed leadership. My main role was to promote racial-ethnic harmony and improve campus safety. Vaughn needed a battlefield sergeant, not an instructional leader. Student achievement was never on the radar screen of anyone, including the parents. Who had time for teaching and learning? Besides, there were no consequences for failing kids.

Staff morale was low, especially during the 1992–1993 school year when all district staff members were notified of a 10 percent pay cut, which followed a 3 percent pay cut from the year before. Waiver applications for increased personnel and fiscal autonomy were rejected by the school district and the teacher's union. A group of teachers began to investigate other means to achieve more flexibility in the operation of our school. Parents of special education students wanted to return their children to the neighborhood school. Instead of the 3Rs, our days were filled with the 3Bs: bus duty, budget constraints, and "but, you can't!"

In November 1992, our school council sent twelve of us to Sacramento for training conducted by Senator Gary Hart and his staff. We were thoroughly enlightened. Though scared by lawyers and district staff, 86 percent of the teachers voted to start the charter application process. We believed that we could do no worse. On July 1, 1993, we became the first independent, urban conversion charter school not only in the state of California but in the nation.

"When no government funds flowed to us in July . . . I mortgaged my house. All staff agreed not to be paid until August."

We had no clue of the hard journey ahead. Skills needed to educate students were never a problem; the problems centered on legal and fiscal liability issues. When no government funds flowed to us in July, when our year-round school began, I mortgaged my house. All staff agreed not to be paid until August.

When local banks refused to set up accounts due to our lack of legal status, we had to manage with our small donation account until the Internal Review Service (IRS) recognized our existence. When the labor unions demanded their monthly dues even when the employees received no paycheck, I took out personal savings to pay all dues. When no reputable insurance company submitted bids for our liability, workers' comp, and health care, we had to accept a lower-rated firm at high premium costs. When the free or reduced-price meal program was threatened, we flew to the nation's capital to beg for approval just one day before school opened.

BUILDING A POWERFUL COALITION

When very few applicants responded to our eleven open teaching positions, Vaughn started classes with seven emergency-permit teachers and four long-term substitutes. When the assistant principal, the plan manager, and seven other classified employees left, we did not fill these positions, because everyone was willing to pick up the slack. Gradually, a coalition developed that included media and legislators, businesses and foundations, universities and organizations.

"We became media savvy immediately. We were a failing inner-city school striving to be independent and accountable. The press portrayed our struggles as a battle between David and Goliath."

MEDIA AND LEGISLATORS

We became media savvy immediately. We were a failing inner-city school striving to be independent and accountable. The press portrayed our struggles with the large Los Angeles Unified School District as a battle between David and Goliath. The *Daily News* and *Los Angeles News* published almost weekly stories as we developed our charter, gained our teacher votes, and battled through the approval process and all the subsequent problems with funding. Even the *Sacramento Bee* tried to defend the defenseless. We were invited to radio talk shows. Television channels joined in the advocacy. We were spotlighted in local news, in a segment by Diane Sawyer on Prime Time, on Good Morning America and national and local PBS stations, and in magazines such as *Time*, *Business Week*, and *Newsweek*.

Our legislative representatives lent us their ears. The first person who came to our rescue was our assemblyman, Richard Katz. He made it clear to the school district that Vaughn was to receive its fair share of the state's education dollars. He or his staff represented us in meetings with the USDA for food services for our students, with the U.S. Department of Education regarding Title I funds, with the Department of the State Architect regarding our new construction, and with district lawyers regarding our right to buy and own land.

I became an instant national spokesperson on the charter school movement. I served as a keynote speaker and have testified at state hearings in more than thirty-two states, including Alaska and Hawaii. In addition, I participated in a small focus group discussion with President Bill Clinton, Vice President Al Gore, Secretary of Education Richard W. Riley, and leaders of the Democratic and Republican parties. A congressional hearing on school reform was held at Vaughn in 1997. Legislators who wanted to sponsor a charter school bill as well as candidates running for local offices visited us. In 1997, Hillary Clinton's visit confirmed that Vaughn was a village fully capable of raising its children.

BUSINESSES AND FOUNDATIONS

Various chambers of commerce and their board members rallied behind our struggles. They wrote letters and op-ed pieces. Their lawyer and accountant members helped us pro bono. The San Fernando Chamber was trying to arrange a loan for us. The League of Women Voters spoke on our behalf in front of the Board of Education. The Valley Industry and Commerce Association adopted official policies in support of us.

Foundations watched our slow but steady efforts in improving the lives of the children and their families. Mayor Richard Riordan donated more than 100 computers and software. The McGraw-Hill Company shipped us obsolete books. Other foundations, including RJR Nabisco, Schwartz Family, Community Technology, Kaiser, and Unihealth, recognized our capacity and funded our grant proposals.

One of the greatest coaches was the Los Angeles Education Partnership. This intermediary helped us create the Family Center and school-linked services. It prompted us to think about the need for a pre-K–12 urban learning center that would provide comprehensive, community-based programs and services.

UNIVERSITIES AND ORGANIZATIONS

Researchers were fascinated with our process. Vaughn participated in various free evaluative studies and long-term case study research. Studies were completed by the Consortium of Policy Research in Education, WestEd, the California Charter Development Center, the National School Reform Center, the Milken Family Foundation, Federal and State After-school Program, and the Nutrition Network. Universities also sent students to conduct observations and to complete master's theses and doctoral dissertations. Professors invited us as class speakers, and they brought classes to Vaughn for on-site visits. Visitors came from Japan, Korea, China, Argentina, Mexico, Chile, New Zealand, and England.

"For 40 years . . . we were to answer to accountability measures established by the state and the district. Now when

external accountability knocks, we don't have to answer. In fact, we're seldom home!"

BUILDING AN INTERNAL ACCOUNTABILITY SYSTEM

The key to our success lies in our ability to build an internal accountability system. For forty years, as an existing public school, we were to answer to accountability measures established by the state and the district. Now, when external accountability knocks, we don't have to answer. In fact, we're seldom home! After the conversion into an independent charter school in 1993, we began to design an internal accountability system that we own and must answer to.

LEADERSHIP ACCOUNTABILITY: SHARED GOVERNANCE AND RESPONSIBILITIES

Vaughn has three working committees with full decision-making authority: the Instruction Committee, the Business Committee, and the Partnership Committee. Each committee consists of twenty members, 50 percent staff and 50 percent parents and community members. All teachers must serve during alternate years. This structure aligns directly with our internal accountability model. This is done to ensure a bottom-up and maximum-inclusion design. This structure also allows us to develop greater organizational capacity, longevity of leadership, equalization of power, and responsibility.

Stable governance supports the goals of the charter; our administrative team has remained intact since the beginning of charter conversion in 1993. This is my eleventh year at Vaughn. No promotion can lure me away, and I will not retire until our new high school is built. As many as twenty-six of the thirty-nine teachers who led the charter school conversion in 1993 are still with us. The entire administrative team remains intact.

TEACHER ACCOUNTABILITY AND PROFESSIONAL GROWTH

We have devised a review and assistance system to help each teacher reach high teaching standards. Areas we stress include lesson planning, classroom management, literacy, language development, special education students in inclusive settings, integration of technology as a teaching and learning tool, mathematics, science, social studies, and arts. We have developed specific rubrics or standards for teachers (especially beginning teachers) for each area.

Systematic staff development that follows is based on observable needs. We have been able to help teachers move up these developmental levels that positively impact students learning. In addition, an elaborate teacher compensation system is linked to demonstrated knowledge and skills. Thus, we have a teacher accountability system that links teaching skills to instructional supervision, to assistance and ongoing evaluation, to precise staff development, and to incentives.

PARENT ACCOUNTABILITY AND FAMILY CAPACITY

Though 69 percent of our parents do not hold a high-school diploma, most of them rise to the occasion when we help each other in building capacity. Our on-site Family Center is a one-stop shop that provides families with basic needs, drop-in counseling, prenatal care, family literacy, a parent exchange service bank, adult education classes, job referrals, and services provided in collaboration with agencies.

"The families and school sign a compact each year. Each family is involved for 30 hours per year in their children's education, for example, by attending parent training . . . or even singing in their church choir."

The families and school sign a compact each year. Each family is involved for thirty hours per year in their children's education, for example, by attending parent training or evening parent forums, taking their children to the public library during vacation, providing child care for another family's sick child, preparing materials at home, participating in neighborhood watch, cleaning up the community, or even singing in their church choir.

As many as thirty parent-educators participate in a Career Ladder and Advanced English-Proficiency Program. Parents may supervise students on the playground, prepare and serve foods in the cafeteria, assist with clerical tasks, or help handicapped students as a one-on-one aide.

EDUCATIONAL ACCOUNTABILITY

In order to carefully and accurately monitor our progress, we measure student achievement using multiple measures and ongoing assessments. Our measurement instruments and practices include the following:

1. California Standardized Assessment Program using Stanford 9.
2. California Professional Development Institute at UCLA, RESULTS Project Assessment, administered three times a year. The project includes a comprehensive, research-based battery of criterion-referenced, diagnostic tests in every skill area of language arts and English language development aligned with state standards. The subtests are given in August, February, and June of each year. Data must be input by teachers and electronically transmitted to UCLA for processing and analysis.
3. Title I multiple measures using SAT9, student report chard rubrics, and writing samples.
4. Los Angeles Unified School District English Learner Profile, with state standards for English language development and redesignation criteria.
5. Our progress is ranked by the state using the Academic Performance Index.

We construct a safety net around students with special needs to ensure the success of all. Proactive activities to end social promotion include a state preschool program beginning at age three, small-group early literacy development, full-day kindergarten, three intersessions (winter warm-up, spring sting, and summer sizzle), tutoring, and cross-grade teaming.

Extended learning opportunities for as many as 600 students include a variety of closely supervised after-school activities daily until 6:00 p.m. Since we serve 119 identified special education students and 844 English learners, we have placed extra efforts in developing and implementing effective process and instruction to meet their needs. These efforts include systematic identification, highly structured service delivery, ongoing monitoring, and follow-up.

Fiscal Accountability

Vaughn has historically been fiscally and operationally sound. We have established sound fiscal standards to ensure financial stability. These standards include the following:

1. Establishing consistent internal control by using effective budgetary and accounting procedures.
2. Completing interim budget projections to make sure that the school is financially sound.
3. Maintaining adequate reserve and cash flow of $2,000,000 in the Los Angeles County Treasury.
4. Reviewing all contracts carefully prior to entering into agreement with vendors and providers.

5. Maintaining comprehensive liability insurance coverage, $15,000,000 per occurrence.
6. Prepaying necessary contracts, liability insurance premiums, and employee health benefit insurance.

For every dollar spent, we consider the students first. A yearly budget is prepared and tentatively adopted each May for the following school year. The Business Committee utilizes a bidding process when needed, tracks its expenditures using computerized programs, reallocates funds, and makes adjustments. We follow systematic accounting practices, with all revenues and expenditures accounted for at all times. All errors are reconciled within a week. Final accounting reports are audited by an independent Certified Public Accountant (CPA). The State Controller's recent four-month comprehensive audit found that we are accountable in all aspects audited.

We continue to make investments through the Los Angeles County Treasury. Currently, we enjoy a cash flow of $4.5 million as well as $2 million in a CD. Paine Webber manages our investment portfolio of $1.2 million. The California Teachers' Credit Union, where we have deposited $500,000, is managing the health benefit expenses of our retirees.

SOLVING THE URBAN SCHOOLING PROBLEMS

Charter school status has given us the opportunity to solve many pressing urban school problems that impact student achievement. These problems include overcrowding and limits to the learning environment, teacher shortage and quality, special education's unfunded mandates, lack of quality preschool, child care and expanded learning opportunities, poor health and nutrition, high-stakes testing, ineffective pre-K–12 education, and the inability of a poor community to support its youths and schools.

OVERCROWDING AND THE LEARNING ENVIRONMENT

Vaughn was the first multitrack year-round school in the northern part of Los Angeles. We operated on a three-track schedule for more than twenty years. Two-thirds of our students (680) were at school while one track (340) stayed home. Siblings were separated; students' language needs were ignored due to scheduling problems and teacher assignment preferences. Our neighborhood does not have theaters, malls, or a library. It is filled with liquor stores and motels.

We also transported 260 students out to other schools due to overcrowding. Teachers had no workroom. There was no space for a computer lab, tutoring, intersession, parent education, or student enrichment. We ended the school year on June 30 and began the new school year on July 1. The district and the state couldn't do anything to help us resolve overcrowding, the lack of an optimal earning environment, or our scheduling nightmare.

Our charter school status has changed all that. We have made the following improvements since charter conversion:

1993: Twenty-two teaching stations, on a sixty/twenty multitrack calendar (year of charter conversion).
1994: Installed six portables and reduced class size to twenty-seven in all grades.
1995: Built Panda Pavilion ($1.2 million) with fourteen new classrooms; installed eight portables; eliminated multi-track schedule; reduced class size to twenty in grades K–3.
1999: Built Panda Village ($3.2 million), with new community library, clinic, museum, multimedia lab, science center, professional development center, and ten demonstration classrooms; reduced class size to twenty in every grade. Vaughn now has seventy-eight teaching stations.
2000: Purchased 2.5 acres across from the school for a 600-seat primary center to house preschool, kindergarten, and grade 1 students. The main campus will then enroll grades six, seven, and eight (expand one grade per year). Anticipated completion date for the PandaLand Primary Center was set for July 2002 (estimated $8 million).
2001: Purchased 3 acres four blocks away for a small 500-student high school academy (Panda Academy) with the focus on training future teachers beginning in grade zero. Anticipated completion date is July 2005 (estimated $10 million).

By 2005, Vaughn will provide 2,500 students with an optimal and personal learning environment on 4 campuses located within a 10-block radius, with approximately 600 students on each campus.

Our capacity building began in 1994. After the first year of the charter school conversion, we realized a $1.2 million surplus from the $4.5 million budget. As a principal of a traditional public school, I had no clue how much it would cost to run my school. The district paid for everything, and the system could not control waste and abuse. Our new internal accountability system demands effective deployment of human and fiscal resources. Savings came from reduced costs in administration, special education, food services, insurance premiums, substitutes, utilities, maintenance, and general purchases. Joint ventures with organizations in delivering health and mental health care added to our savings, as did parent volunteer hours.

"With $600,000 of our savings, we turned a crack house into a school house with fourteen classrooms in less than ten months."

With $600,000 of our savings, we turned a crack house into a school house with fourteen classrooms in less than ten months. We awarded the project to a local contractor. The bid specified the requirement of hiring at least 70 percent of the labor locally, giving preference to our parents who are in the construction trades, including reformed gang members living in the neighborhood as apprentices, and using district high school students in a career-to-work program (Federal Perkins) to build the cabinets. Not only is this a cost-saving strategy, but we have provided jobs in the community and training to at-risk youths. Our students stared with pride at their parents doing electrical work and at their siblings doing the plastering. Vandalism and theft are nonexistent at Vaughn.

In 1996, California began its class size reduction program. The state provided $650 for each student (K–3) in a class with a pupil-to-teacher ratio of 20:1 and $40,000 for each classroom built or leased for the purpose of class size reduction. With such a substantial reimbursement from the state, we paid off our first building within one year. Through shrewd reinvestment and timely land purchases, we went on to build the second building and have paid it off. We still have $4.5 million in our building fund.

We have solved the overcrowding problem. We can accommodate 1,350 students with a class size of twenty in each class. Busing is reduced to fourteen students. We are the only school in Los Angeles to eliminate the multi-track calendar and offer 200 school days per year. There are rooms for three computer labs, a teacher resource center, a site-based clinic and counseling center, a large multipurpose room for fine arts, a piano studio, a museum, a large science lab, a large library with seventeen books per student, a special education infant room, three resource rooms, and space for child care, parent education, and community activities during school hours.

We are now able to provide space for district training, including school nurse CPR training, special education workshops, beginning teacher seminars, and early childhood make-and-take workshops at no cost to the district. Two universities hold their credential classes at Vaughn: UCLA and CSUN. A small rental lease is paid, and our beginning teachers may take some of these mandatory credentialing classes tuition free. Community organizations and governmental entities including the Department of Justice are now housed at Vaughn. It is now a village bigger than Hillary Clinton had envisioned.

We contract with the district for routine repair by paying 2 percent of our base revenues. By helping the district pass a citywide bond fund (Proposition

BB) and agreeing to provide a small percentage of match dollars, we have received $1.4 million worth of network infrastructure upgrade, E-rate support, modernization of the main office, and various technology and safety projects. In collaboration with Fenton Avenue Charter School and the district, we applied for and received $3.8 million from the Federal Qualified Zone Academy Bond, an interest-free loan with a twelve-year term. We used the funds for modernization, repair, and equipment purchase. In the meantime, the bond funds are accruing interest.

TEACHER SHORTAGE AND TEACHER QUALITY

Without union contract constraints and district personnel policies, we are able to assertively recruit and retain qualified teachers. We now have sixty-nine teachers, fourteen with a master's degree, 19 percent on emergency permit, and thirty-eight certified bilingual teachers. The turnover rate is 7 percent to 8 percent each year. Tools are provided for every teacher to succeed.

Teaching Environment and School Culture. Our teachers form teams of three teachers responsible for sixty students. Each team consists of an experienced teacher with ten or more years of teaching experience. He or she is partnered with a teacher with three to five years of experience and one emergency-credentialed, beginning teacher. Each team establishes team goals. The focused, targeted collaboration includes frequent communication, weekly planning, a search for common solutions, mutual support, and help to reach collective goals.

Our teachers can share full-time positions in various ways, including a four-day work week, one-semester assignment, and a six- to ten-week positive switch between a general and a special education teacher. Every two grade levels have a resource specialist and an instructional coordinator. This structure strengthens the schoolwide teamwork.

Paraprofessionals with a teaching career goal are provided with a flexible work schedule and sufficient compensation so they can complete their studies in a timely manner. Each year, two or three qualified paraprofessionals are selected to fill vacant teacher positions. Often, the experienced teachers who train them become their team leaders. Our preschool and Head Start teachers are guaranteed elementary teaching positions upon completion of elementary certification requirements. Teachers have ample opportunities to rotate the other grade levels and subjects within our pre-K–12 structure. In addition, teachers with specific expertise such as special education, technology, or English language development can teach university courses at Vaughn. Both UCLA and the California State University–Northridge schedule eight different credential classes on campus in the evening and during weekends.

Teacher Training and Professional Growth. Our teachers have developed a set of teaching standards related to lesson planning, classroom management, and various subject areas that are linked to the students' learning standards. Levels of performance in each area are clearly described using a four-point scale with descriptive rubrics (for details, visit our website: www.vaughn.k12.ca.us).

We replaced the state teacher evaluation system with our Peer Assistance and Review System that takes place four times per year. Our teachers reflect on their own performance and rate themselves using the established teaching standards and scoring rubrics. Selected peer reviewers observe their colleagues and provide feedback as well as assistance. Instructional coordinators also conduct classroom visits and confer with teachers on an ongoing basis. Beginning teachers are assigned one-to-one mentors. Elected grad-level chairpersons are responsible for ensuring that teachers understand and focus on grade-level standards. The director of instruction and I conduct weekly visits, monitor progress of beginning teachers, and focus on schoolwide goals.

Based on an individual teacher's performance review, teachers are provided with differentiated training. Training opportunities include small-group workshops, individualized conferencing, observing another teacher, participating in seminars, conducting research, using technology, and pairing with a teacher buddy. We generally spend 5 percent of our base revenue in staff development (approximately $200,000 per year).

Teachers must base teaching decisions on solid data rather than on assumptions. Data help us monitor and assess student performance. The governor's Professional Development Institute provided results-focused programs for 70,000 teachers this year. We captured the opportunity, and all our teachers participated in UCLA's Focusing on Results training at no cost to us. Our teachers were paid by the institute to attend.

> **"In addition to base pay and extra compensation for certification and advanced degrees, teachers receive skills and knowledge pay, contingency-based awards, schoolwide student achievement bonuses, expertise compensation, gainsharing, and other benefits."**

Teacher Compensation. The single-salary pay plan does not support standards-based instruction and does not work for Vaughn. In an effort to recruit and retain quality teachers, we developed a performance pay plan. In addition to base pay and extra compensation for certification and advance degrees, teachers receive skills and knowledge pay, contingency-based awards, schoolwide student achievement bonuses, expertise compensation, gainsharing, and other benefits.

Skills and Knowledge Pay. Level 1 skills include literacy, language arts, mathematics, working with special education students in an inclusive setting, classroom management, and lesson planning. A score of 2.5 or higher in the performance review earns $4,500. An overall score of 3.0 in other subject matters (social studies, science, arts, English language learning, physical education) earns another $5,300. Any fully credentialed teacher whose average in all of the areas is 3.5 or higher earns an additional $4,500. The maximum in bonuses that a teacher can earn by getting top scores on every part of the knowledge and skills review is $14,300.

Contingency-Based Awards. Teachers can earn a total of $2,000 a year for achieving certain goals in the areas of student attendance, discipline, parental involvement, and working in teams.

Schoolwide Student Achievement Bonuses. All teachers and administrators get an annual bonus of $1,500 if the school as a whole meets the Academic Performance Index (API) goal set by the state, regardless of how much the state provides. Noncertificated staff and part-time staff members also earn a prorated amount.

Expertise Compensation. Teachers in a leadership role, including grade-level chair, committee chair, peer reviewer, mentor, and faculty representative, receive additional stipends. A teacher who sponsors after-school clubs, student government, or field learning or who teaches intersession is compensated $3,500 to $4,000.

Gainsharing. Unused sick days continue to accrue, and $235 is provided for every ten unused days as an attendance award. A separate investment account with more than $1,000,000 is set up to guarantee these bonuses. Teachers share the accrued interest as a form of stock option. The amount is estimated at $1,000 per year per teacher. Based on payroll records (excluding expertise pay), a first-year fully credentialed teacher earns $46,000. A first-year emergency-credentialed teacher earns $39,000. A teacher with ten years of teaching experience and average scores of 3.0 earns $63,850.

Added Benefits. To provide a further sense of security, we have purchased a long-term disability insurance policy for every teacher which provides 60 percent of their full pay till age sixty-five. In addition, we have set up an account with $500,000 in the Los Angeles Teachers' Credit Union to guarantee health benefits after retirement. We are in the process of developing further benefits for teachers, including college and child care subsidies, and cash reimbursement for out-of-pocket purchases for classroom use.

Not only have we solved the teacher shortage problem, but we have built a highly qualified, cohesive, and dedicated teaching corps. Most recently we accepted veteran teachers who resigned from the district to transfer to Vaughn. This team led Vaughn to win the California Distinguished Schools Award in 1996 and the National Blue Ribbon Schools Award in 1997. As many as 154 of us went to Washington, DC, to accept the award in 1997. In 2001, as many as eighty-four teachers and support staff went to China, with all expenses paid. We spent eleven days together, teaching at three schools in Beijing and Shanghai. There's a huge sense of pride and accomplishment.

SPECIAL EDUCATION AND UNFUNDED MANDATES

Every district in the nation is seeking better ways to meet the mandates of the Individuals with Disabilities Education Act (IDEA). Public schools must serve special education students effectively without huge encroachment costs to general education. As a traditional public school, Vaughn was totally out of compliance while costing the district huge encroachment costs. As an independent charter school, we are fully responsible for all the special education students attending Vaughn.

We are implementing a unique inclusion program staffed with three certified special education resource specialists, three special education assistants, and a team of seven support personnel. We make accurate identifications, forge close collaborations between the general education and the special education teachers, and maintain positive relationships with parents. Our inclusion program serves eighty-seven identified special education students (mild and severe). They are meeting their IEP goals in a timely manner in an inclusive learning environment.

We entered into a revenue-neutral agreement with the district. Vaughn receives all the funds for special education and is committed to serve all identified special education students living in the pre-charter geographic boundary. For low-incidence students whom we can't serve, we contract with the district and pay for the costs. We make every effort to keep our special education students at Vaughn by providing our teachers and families with the needed support. We are meeting all IDEA provisions with success with minimum excess costs.

ACCESS TO PRESCHOOL EDUCATION AND QUALITY CHILD CARE

Children in our community need an early start, but our parents can't afford the costs. There is no licensed child care center in our neighborhood other than a district-operated Children's Center that has a multi-year waiting list. A state Desegregation Program provided only ninety spaces for four-year-olds four days per week and two and a half hours per day. The majority of our students stayed home with no early childhood education opportunities.

In 1998, we read about the universal preschool strategy discussed by the State Department of Education and the expansion of state preschool in poor neighborhoods. The Los Angeles Unified School District received an expansion grant but was short of space. With our flexibility as a charter school, we collaborated with the district by converting the desegregation-funded classes to a licensed preschool with eight state preschool sessions, four in the morning serving eighty students and four in the afternoon serving another eighty students, five days per week, three hours per day. We can even enroll three-year olds in the afternoon, many of whom are students with some identified disabilities. The school district passes the grant funds to us and withholds 4 percent for administrative costs.

When we learned that the Los Angeles County Office of Education was administering the expansion of the federal Head Start program, we made use of the opportunity to further strengthen our preschool program. The new initiative focuses on locating the program in elementary school sites where the articulation with formal schooling can take place. We are the first elementary site with such a wrap-around program, using our charter school flexibility. We now have four sessions of Head Start serving the same afternoon state preschool children till 6:00 p.m. These younger and developmentally delayed children now receive six and a half hours of daily instruction and language development. We now serve as the model site for a unique, universal preschool education program.

LACK OF EXPANDED LEARNING OPPORTUNITIES

Prior to charter conversion, we kept our playground open as a voluntary, permissive after-school child care program from 2:25 to 4:25 p.m. daily. We had 2 playground workers for as many as 400 students on certain days. There were no organized sports or clubs. Our charter school status now allows us to apply as a local educational agency (LEA) for competitive after-school grants. In 1999, we won the Federal 21st-Century Community Learning Center Grant, the State Safe School and Neighborhood Grant, and the city-funded LA BEST Program. All three revenue sources now support a well-organized after-school program for as many as 600 students, with daily tutoring, homework support, sports, and 16 interest clubs.

As an LEA, we applied for the state Early Literacy and Accelerated English Learning Grant, which provides intensive intersession instruction to ELD students. We have been funding twenty extra instructional days for three years, and now the state is funding what we started.

LACK OF HEALTH CARE AND NUTRITION

Due to poverty and lack of documentation, many of our students do not receive adequate health care. We built a little on-site clinic and convinced the Los Angeles County Health Department to provide primary care services to all Vaughn students and their siblings up to age eighteen. A team of nurse practitioners, a doctor, and medical assistants are on-site daily, providing immunizations, CHDP, blood and urine tests, health education, medication, treatment for communicable diseases, and referral to the nearby ULCA/Olive View Hospital for critical care.

The program is funded by a federal match grant to the county for its dollar-for-dollar expenditures on health care in Empowerment Zone communities. The focus is to offer primary care at school sites and reduce costs for emergency care at county-operated hospitals. Vaughn provides the facilities and in-kind costs for utilities, maintenance, a part-time school nurse, and a health advocate. After six months of infrastructure building and operation, the Unihealth Foundation agreed to assume our in-kind costs.

Often, the school meals are the only meals our students receive throughout the day. In an effort to provide more nutritious meals and more choices of healthful foods within the same USDA Child Nutrition budget, we took over the operation from the district beginning in 1994. Since 95 percent of our students qualify for free or reduced-priced meals, we take advantage of a new policy offered by the USDA. Students apply once every four years, as a base year. During the subsequent years, paperwork is kept to a minimum. This universal feeding program eliminates the loss of valuable instructional time while trimming costs. All students are provided three free meals daily; breakfast, lunch, and a late snack. They have five choices of entrees, fruits, and vegetables.

Last year, we were admitted to the Nutrition Network as a separate public entity. The Network, through the State Department of Health, provides match grants for nutrition education, health awareness projects, and community outreach efforts. Our in-kind budget spent on health- and nutrition-related programs leverages approximately $25,000 per year from the Network. More importantly, our students and their families now receive additional health and nutrition services.

HIGH-STAKES TESTING AND SANCTIONS

In 1996, our standardized test scores dipped because of the inclusion of all special education students as well as English learners with low English proficiency levels. Such departure from the norm resulted in many negative comments regarding our academic accountability. But in 1997, our test scores improved. Later, the state of California passed Proposition 227 and required that all English learners take the SAT 9. We were ahead of the curve.

> **"As a charter school, we are in a fish bowl. When an anonymous phone call . . . alleged cheating, we were on the front page . . . for months. . . . At the end of five months, we were exonerated."**

As a charter school, we are in a fishbowl. When an anonymous phone call to the district office alleged cheating, we were on the front page of both local newspapers for months. Four teachers were investigated by the district. We called in a team from McGraw-Hill and the UCLA Assessment Center to readminister another standardized test (Terra Nova) to cross-validate our student achievement. At the end of five months, additional expenses, and investigative sessions, we were exonerated.

We must develop and implement alternative and multiple assessments so we won't be subjected to SAT 9 testing only and the subsequent sanctions when applied. For two years, we administered an additional standardized pre- and post-testing (Terra Nova) in addition to the SAT 9. External proctors from UCLA were assigned to each class, and data were analyzed by McGraw-Hill. In addition, three times per year, we administer block testing on reading and math and collect writing samples. Each student has a portfolio of work that goes from teacher to teacher throughout the student's educational years at Vaughn.

Beginning in 2000–2001, as the entire district focuses on Open Court and Success for All, we have the autonomy to participate in the Governor's Initiative on standards and assessment. We began to transition to a comprehensive instructional and assessment system (Focus on Results) managed by the UCLA Professional Development Center at no cost to us.

We met our 1999–2000 SPI goal and received a monetary award from the state. Instead of issuing $591.32 to each full-time staff member, we offered $1,500 each as part of the guarantee of our performance pay program. To continue the incentive even when the state discontinues the award, we will provide every teacher with $2,000 each year if together we meet the future API goals.

LACK OF COMMUNITY RESOURCES

Urban schools compete for limited community resources. Low-income communities have a hard time supporting their members and children. We utilize our charter autonomy and flexibility to help build a healthier and even wealthier community.

For instance, we forged a partnership with a neighborhood for-profit dump site to build a community library on our campus to illustrate social injustice. Our site-based clinic provides health care, and our counseling center staffed with outsourced personnel from nonprofit agencies helps many families deal with various social realities. Our Family Center provides a one-stop shop for social services, including food and clothing, housing assistance, employment referrals, taxi coupons, and prenatal care. Adult classes are on-site during the day and evening, and we have a Media Center for computer training.

We bought as many dilapidated buildings and cracked houses as possible. By building new schools, we beautify the community and provide many jobs. Property values in the neighborhood have gone up. UCLA and California State University–Northridge established a Professional Development Center and offer teacher credentialing classes during the week and on weekends. Our future Business Co-Op operated by the parents will add economic development to our neighborhood. Little by little, our community begins to look like a learning village, with Vaughn as its anchor.

> **"We witnessed our fourteen-year-old former students becoming pregnant and our fifteen-year-olds joining gangs. We decided to . . . provide a seamless pre-K–12 education at Vaughn. . . . Since two universities are already on campus, Vaughn can easily develop into a pre-K–16 learning center."**

DISCONNECTED PRE-K–12 EDUCATION

We are saddened whenever our graduates, especially those with special education needs, do not succeed in the large neighborhood middle and high schools. There is little articulation between elementary, middle, and high school levels. Every school stays in its box and maintains its turf. In fact, there is frequent finger-pointing among the three levels. We witnessed our fourteen-year-old former students becoming pregnant and our fifteen-year-olds joining gangs.

We decided to build a middle school and a high school to provide a seamless pre-K–12 education at Vaughn. Our instructional program will be well articulated throughout the grades, all under one leadership team with a collective mission and vision. The four campuses (primary center, elementary, middle school, and high school academy), with 600 students in each, will be within walking distance of each other. High school students can mentor the middle school students, who in turn can tutor the elementary peers who will assist the preschool teachers. It is our goal to usher every graduate to a postsecondary education. Vaughn will have ample internal human capital to make sure that every child succeeds. Since the universities are already on campus, Vaughn can easily develop into a pre-K–16 learning center when opportunities allow.

Our consistent strategy is to redeploy our human and fiscal resources to meet the needs of our students as we research the educational and political trends that match our programs. Then, in a timely manner, we lobby or compete for the resources targeted for these programs. We have never failed, not once. Even if we don't implement certain programs ourselves, other organizations will be knocking at our door.

THE AMERICAN URBAN SCHOOL DREAM

In 1993, we were given a license to dream. The dream is not about power, wealth, and status; it is about opportunities to solve urban schooling problems that we have faced for over forty years. It's the American Urban School Dream. For eight long years, we pursued this dream with all our passion, energy, enthusiasm, teamwork, and newrly learned skills. We are now a successful full-service, community-based public charter school that turned mission impossible into mission possible.

"Our relationship with the (school district) was very difficult during the first three years. . . . We consistently challenged their existing practices."

Our relationship with the Los Angeles Unified School District was very difficult during the first three years of charter conversion. We consistently challenged their existing practices and pushed reform to its limits. After we built capacity and proved our worth, the district adopted new policies that we have set in place, including the USDA Universal Child Nutrition Program, per-pupil budgeting, special education inclusion, the Qualified Zone Academy Bond Project, and various activities to end social promotion.

In addition, the district has contracted with Vaughn for state preschool, modernization of existing school buildings, special education services, and beginning teacher training. Vaughn was also asked to provide guidance to the District Accountability Team regarding performance-based evaluation. Most recently, I participated in the district committee to adopt criteria for the selection of the new superintendent. When Vaughn speaks, the district listens.

Chapter 4

New Leaders on the Block

Vaughn Next Century Learning Center, 2019

From its rather abrupt beginning in 1993 as the first conversion school to change to charter status in the United States, Vaughn quickly evolved from a long-time low-performing, over-crowded, traditional elementary school built in 1950 in the Los Angeles Unified School District to a California Distinguished School and National Blue Ribbon School (repeatedly designated) within the first decade of its transformation.

Beginning with the elementary campus on Vaughn Street in San Fernando Valley, Vaughn Next Century Learning Center now spans five campuses serving over 3,200 students from pre-K through grade twelve (and even more parents and community members in additional facilities). Their property purchases in the vicinity allowed them to expand to include several additional facilities in Pacoima, and while it has not been their aim to grow, they continue to do so due to demand. The institution has transformed from the "New Kid on the Block" elementary school to the not so "Little School that Could," and it definitely does. Its website depicts the growth of the organization:

1993—Vaughn Street Elementary was converted to charter status and renamed Vaughn Next Century Learning Center. It has since become named Mainland and houses fourth, fifth, and some sixth grade students (13330 Vaughn Street).

2000—The Middle School of International Studies & Technology (MIT) became operational. This campus is on the property directly next to the original campus and the building is connected. During the sixth, seventh, and eight grade years in the middle school, students learn study skills, academics, and begin serious preparation for college.

2003—The School Readiness Center, Pandaland, opened serving pre-K students directly across the street from the original campus (13421 Vaughn

Street). Here students as young as three years old learn to read, to do math, to create, and to make friends.

2008—The Vaughn International Studies Academy (VISA) opened, also across the street from the original campus (11505 Herrick Avenue). The high school is made up of multiple pathways to prepare students for college and for future careers that may not yet exist. All students become proficient in academics and communication skills, become good thinkers and team players, become multilingual, and graduate digitally and globally competent.

2012—The Elementary Language Academy for a Global & Green Generation (G3) opened a few blocks from the original campus (11200 Herrick Avenue). In this school, second and third graders learn in pods rather than classrooms, and teachers work in teams to ensure that every student becomes English proficient before moving on to the Mainland. At the Mainland, fourth, fifth, and some sixth graders learn research skills and problem solving and present projects with partners.

Three learning pods were added to the original conversion campus to serve some middle school students in 2014 and additional pods have been added to Pandaland (serving PK–first), the G3 campus (serving second and third), the Mainland (serving fourth, fifth, and some sixth), and the high school to serve their ever-expanding enrollment. A Family Center is located directly across the street from G3 (11201 Herrick Avenue). In addition, Vaughn Central (a new business office to support the growing Vaughn organization) was opened in 2016 to help administer the five campuses. This building stands between the two larger campus sites. The whole of the Vaughn properties are referred to by community members as "an oasis" in the area, having created an educator corridor that runs between Vaughn Street and Herrick Avenue. (Some parents are now asking for a college.)

"From its rather abrupt beginning in 1993 as the first conversion school to change to charter status in the United States, Vaughn quickly evolved from a long-time low-performing, over-crowded, traditional elementary school built in 1950 in the Los Angeles Unified School District to a California Distinguished School and National Blue Ribbon School (repeatedly designated) within the first decade of its transformation."

To say that this first conversion charter school in the country has been a success would be a gross understatement. Addressing exactly how they have accomplished all this would have to start with their original leader, Dr. Yvonne Chan, and while her story of the Vaughn Next Century Learning Center adventure in the prior chapter reveals much of her tireless tenacity and a driven sense of purpose, she is too humble to attribute the tremendous success of Vaughn to herself or her leadership. Fortunately, multiple outside sources shed light on this story and point to the critical role of her strong leadership in the continued success of Vaughn.

YVONNE CHAN

Dr. Chan was born and raised in China and immigrated to the United States alone at the age of seventeen with $100 in her pocket. She attributes her initial success to the public education system in the country. She earned a degree from UCLA and then a school administrative credential from California State University at Northridge. She was a teacher for sixteen years before moving into school leadership. She was a successful principal prior to coming to Vaughn, and LAUSD moved her to troubled schools as somewhat of a turnaround principal.

Dr. Chan was assigned as principal of Vaughn Street School in 1990, a time when the area was deeply gang infested; there was even a dead body found in front of the school one day. Teachers had filed grievances, and there was a general climate of hopelessness. She decided her first task was to put an aesthetically pleasing retainer wall around the campus and plant some grass to make the school somewhat more inviting. She claims that she "required" the neighborhood to help her build this school border, and they did, evidence of her strong leadership.

At the same time, across the street from the project, she said she served Budweiser and Coors Light to the volunteer parents. In twenty years, the school district had been unable to accomplish this school border, but the quick success on this community project gave the stakeholders hope and confidence that change could happen at Vaughn with Dr. Chan at the helm.

"To say that this first conversion charter school in the country has been a success would be a gross understatement."

Then California passed Senate Bill # 1448 in 1992, allowing schools to change their status to charter and take more control over all aspects of the school functions from finances to curriculum. When interviewed in 2011, long-time California senator Gary Hart explained:

My original vision was for charters to be a creative alternative within public education—an "R & D" (Research and Development) lab, if you will, from which policy makers and educators could, on occasion, gain valuable insights. In addition, I have always had a strong belief that no one has a corner on educational excellence and that some significant educational variety in a state as large and as diverse as California was a good thing, and charters could help promote such variety. Finally, I knew that some parents felt their local schools were not meeting their children's needs and providing an alternative to such parents (besides private and parochial schools), I felt, was important.[1]

Chan had already begun to infuse some hope into Vaughn Elementary, but the new legislation gave her and her community the mechanism through which they could dream bigger. She immediately gathered the teachers who were interested, brought together the local parents, and mobilized a team to write a charter and take advantage of the "wonderful new legislation" that California had passed. She saw moving to charter status as an opportunity to help people who may have been overlooked or failed by the system to thrive through a similar yet different system in the future. She claimed that first and foremost, all of her stakeholders needed the right attitude, and the students always came first, always.

Chan's fire and grit is partially evidenced through her actions reported in her own story in the preceding chapter, through her tireless tenacity and extraordinary strength of purpose. When she was inducted into the Charter School Hall of Fame in 2008, parents, teachers, students, and even other principals whom she has influenced shared testimonials that speak to her leadership.

"You're not just another student to her. She knows our names. She recognizes who you are, what you've done." "She has never seen any obstacle as an obstacle, she sees obstacles as opportunities." "She's like a little red hot pepper. You bite into a pepper, it's spicy, but it doesn't go away. It keeps on going." In her own words, Chan states, "We convince each other there's hope." "As we join forces, there's that confidence." "We change people's mindset, culture, build hope and confidence and see that things can change." Her natural and repeated expression of the pronoun "we" reveals that not only does she inspire others, but she is inspired by the combined work of the team.[2]

ANITA ZEPEDA

As Vaughn's success story spread and states across the country began to consider their own charter legislation, Chan was invited to speak to legislatures in thirty-seven states. At this point, new leadership was needed for the day to day running of the enlarged Vaughn organization so that Yvonne could serve as an ambassador for the movement. Fortunately, Chan had been busy cultivating leadership for the future of Vaughn all along the way.

Anita Zepeda had a general education credential from California State University at Northridge, and after teaching for a while she became interested in helping children better break the code of literacy. She started taking classes and wound up with a Special Education Credential, then after that, a Reading Credential. Anita had worked with Yvonne long before Chan even came to Vaughn.

Anita had been an administrator at a school where Yvonne was a teacher. She recalls one day long ago when Yvonne came into her office with a little Apple computer, filled with exciting ideas of what this little machine might bring to an educational setting such as classrooms. Yvonne was soon reassigned to another school, and Anita moved on to become division advisor of Special Education within LAUSD, a district office position, but the two women stayed in touch.

> **"She recalls a high level district officer asking her, 'Anita, are you sure you want to do this? . . . Join this crazy woman?' Her decision was made. She did!"**

Then in 1993, Zepeda got a call from her former colleague. Chan was excited about the possibility of turning Vaughn into a charter, and she wanted Zepeda to come aboard to help with Special Education. As it was, the timing was perfect. Anita had tired of the slow-moving district office operation and truly "missed the kids." She had harbored a dream to try a full-inclusion model in practice in a school, and Chan assured her that this is what she would like to see at Vaughn. She recalls a high-level district officer asking her, "Anita, are you *sure* you want to do this? Go back to being a resource teacher? Join this crazy woman?" Her decision was made. She did!

So Anita Zepeda was aboard *The Little Engine That Could* right from the ground floor. At the time, Vaughn had only identified seventeen students as needing Special Education services, and they were bussed out to another school. She found, however, that *many* more students clearly had disabilities; they just had not been identified. Once changing to charter status, they tried to avoid placing labels of any kind on students. The new vision for the school would ensure that every child would receive the services they needed without an IEP.

So in the beginning, some of the neighborhood children with special needs were brought back to Vaughn. Little by little the program there became a full inclusion program, and Anita's dream was realized. After a summer symposium on early education training, Zepeda decided she may be ready to take on another leadership role within the primary grades. While there was no charter money for pre-K at charter schools, there was a state pre-K program that Vaughn was able to tap into and create Pandaland. They reapply for this funding every year. Since pre-K has its own set of specifications and regulations, they built their primary center with PK on the ground floor and TK and kindergarten on the second floor. Thus Anita's leadership journey continued.

When asked about Chan's leadership, Zepeda said, "Dr. Chan won't ask her staff to do something that she wouldn't do herself. There is nothing that she wouldn't do for her kids. She doesn't wait for resources to come to her, she seeks them out. She has been a wonderful mentor to all of us."[3] Eventually, Yvonne convinced Anita to get a school leadership administrative credential, and she did that as well.

In 2008, the year that the high school became operational, Chan was being asked to speak all over the country, and the school leadership and the board all agreed that Anita was the perfect leader to fill in the role of executive director of Vaughn Next Century Learning Center. When asked about the differences between her leadership and Yvonne's, Zepeda said, "We really balance each other. I'm close to the community; I build relationships—actually I guess we're similar that way—we both pick up trash, paint, do whatever needs to be done. But I could never be Yvonne on facilities. She writes all those grants and contracts. I'm more focused on the instructional part. I was always more focused on the curriculum and instruction, and Yvonne was more focused on the business connections, getting funders, etc."

Anita is particularly proud of the accomplishments of the high school program that began in 2008. Just in time to celebrate its twenty-fifth year anniversary as a charter, the high school campus received a Silver Award in 2017 from the *US News and World Report*, having received a Bronze Award the year prior. Vaughn International Studies High School has successfully served a 99 percent minority student profile (of 2,724), with a 97 percent economically disadvantaged student population, and with a 97 percent graduation rate in that year of students who began in their high school and 92 percent overall. Using the term "International" in the title of the campus is not just a word. The Vaughn high school students travel to China and host students from China annually. The staff travels frequently as well.

"Anita is particularly proud of the accomplishments of the high school program that began in 2008."

Zepeda explained that as the school grew to five campuses, the staff by necessity became less connected with each other. While the high school and middle school worked fairly closely, the high school folks didn't really know the second- and third-grade people. In addition, there are large teams of support personnel such as counselors, psychologists, and social workers at each level and closer connections between the groups were more effective and efficient. They feared that they were losing their closeness as a staff that they had enjoyed in the 1990s on the single site.

In addition, as the planning for the high school was progressing, they looked at each other and realized that few of them had been very far outside of the San Fernando Valley, much less overseas. They wondered how they could truly develop a high school with a global focus. To address these concerns, they began intensive training and included travel as part of that training. Zepeda shared, "In the early days, we ate breakfast and lunch together. We worked long hard hours together. Now we needed to step out and travel together to interact and build relationships among the professionals at the different levels."

They went to Germany and Poland in 2017 because they wanted to see Birkenau and Auschwitz. They are celebrating their twenty-fifth anniversary by 160 staff members going to Greece together. When asked how they fund this, Anita shared that the foundation collects some funding from the visiting international students, and staff members pay 50 percent of their travel costs. They travel over spring break so that there is no lost work time. They do not just talk about being global and international, they are living it.

They have also learned to be "shovel ready." While there is no specified intent to grow, when property comes available, they have learned that it is wise to purchase it if possible. The original site only houses fourth and fifth graders presently. Some of the original bungalows had been on LAUSD property, so over time they agreed to split the cost 50/50. They bought repurposed cargo bins which were bigger than the bungalows and put in a lot of grass and a garden center to create a much more esthetically pleasing and functional facility. They bought a nearby house that had gone on the market to hold washers, driers, and bathing facilities for their homeless students; all of which matches perfectly with their mission of being solely focused on the children.

They continue to build their mental health teams within the different grade levels, and teachers do home visits to build relationships with families. They are not critical or judgmental but make clear to the community that Vaughn professionals are engaged in a labor of love and are there to help. A recent complexity has been children arriving home from school to find one or both of their parents deported. Consequently, they are educating their parents on filling out affidavits to help ensure their children continue to be educated regardless of home circumstances.

Anita shared that as this chapter goes to press, she has decided to retire after twenty-five years at Vaughn Next Century Learning Center (combined with many years in the public school system prior). She says she will remain in a consulting role and help with the transition for the new leader just as Yvonne has done. She points out that one cannot always find institutional memory in a document, and she wants to be absolutely sure that the mission of Vaughn continues seamlessly.

When asked what they are looking for in their next leader, she stated that "heart is #1! This community needs this. It is heart that keeps you going in the hard times and keeps you going. It's sort of like those qualities from the *Wizard of Oz*; with wisdom, the courage to make decisions, and heart guiding it all, everything else falls into place. You just stay focused on the kids. That's what drives us."

"Vaughn professionals are engaged in a labor of love and are there to help."

As Dr. Chan was accepting an award from the Center for Educational Reform in 2013, she retold her story of coming to America (American means "golden mountain" in Chinese) and stated that she did not realize "the true American dream until 1993, after 22 years of working for a bureaucratic blob. . . . The charter was my license to dream. It was affirmation that there is life, liberty and the pursuit of happiness." She also promised to continue to "outrun the blob" until her last "dying breath."

NOTES

1. "Getting to Know: Senator Gary K. Hart, Author of the California Charter Schools Act." California Charter Schools Association, accessed January 12, 2020 at http://library.ccsa.org/blog/2011/05/getting-to-know-senator-gary-k-hart-author-of-the-california-charter-schools-act.html.

2. "Yvonne Chan Hall of Fame Award 2008," accessed January 12, 2020 at https://www.youtube.com/watch?v=L1yMIRhP0_M.

3. "Educational Excellence in America," accessed January 12, 2020 at http://www.casablanca-productions.com/Educational2.html.

Chapter 5

Clawing Your Way

By Joe Lucente

On January 1, 1994, Fenton Avenue Elementary School became California's thirtieth charter school and one of the few that were totally autonomous. Fenton Avenue Charter School was one of the largest public elementary charter schools in the nation in the early 2000s, and became a nationally recognized model of a conversion charter school, that is, one that underwent a change from a traditional public school to a public charter school.

Joe Lucente, co-director of Fenton Avenue Charter School, had been a teacher and administrator with the Los Angeles Unified School District for twenty years and has helped guide the school along a successful path of conversion. The school won a 1997 California Distinguished School award, and Lucente was one of five charter school directors from across the nation invited to the White House in August 1998 for a conference sponsored by then First Lady Hillary Rodham Clinton and the Department of Education for new D.C. charter schools.

Lucente was born to immigrant Italian American parents in Renton, Washington. He has lived, gone to school, and worked in Los Angeles most of his life. His employment background included being an administrative officer in the United States Air Force, three-plus years in management positions with the Los Angeles Herald-Examiner, *and thirty-two years in education (two of them abroad). This following story was written by Lucente in 2004.*

In August 1987, I was one of two assistant principals (AP) at a very large, year-round elementary school in Pacoima, California. Pacoima is very much the inner city of the San Fernando Valley, with a predominantly minority population at very low socioeconomic levels. I was working under the tutelage of a very competent and knowledgeable principal, and I was very happy, but I was learning as fast and as much as possible because I knew my time was coming.

Due to an acute shortage of administrators in the Los Angeles Unified School District, capable assistant principals were being promoted after two years of experience. I was now a veteran of twenty months with a name well known in LAUSD because of two older sisters who were longtime successful LAUSD administrators. I didn't have to wait long! I was summoned to the region superintendent's office on a Friday afternoon in mid-August. As my principal put it, the good news was that I was being given a principalship. The bad news was that it was a very "difficult" assignment, about two miles east of my current school. Undaunted by my principal's bad news, I set out to meet my new challenge.

"I was told that Fenton was a school totally out of control, and that I was to be the fifth principal of the school in six years."

The one-and-a-half-hour meeting that followed with the superintendent and region administrator bordered on the bizarre. The majority of the time was spent describing what the superintendent called a "hellhole" known as Fenton Avenue Elementary School—my new assignment! I listened in disbelief. I thought they must be exaggerating to make a point. I was told that Fenton was a school totally out of control, and that I was to be the fifth principal of the school in six years:

- Number one left after nine years during which the school's demographics changed from predominantly African American to predominantly Hispanic.
- Number two died after eighteen months.
- Number three was asked to leave after one year that was punctuated by numerous death threats from a parent!
- Number four sat in his office an entire year with the door closed and a large "No Admittance" sign on it. He relinquished control of the school to a fifth grade teacher new to our district.
- Number five was lucky me!

Fenton was rife with racial problems, theft, vandalism, high student and staff absenteeism, frequent fights among students, staff, parents, and community members, single-digit test scores, financial mismanagement, and every other sign of a totally dysfunctional school! I was informed it was one of the two worst schools in the San Fernando Valley. (To understand the magnitude of that statement, one must realize that if the San Fernando Valley were a school district, it would be the seventh largest in the nation. It is also of note that the other of the two worst schools was Vaughn Street Elementary School.)

To make matters worse, the region administrator who recommended me for the position informed me that I was her last hope because her last several promotes had failed. "You must succeed. I'm counting on you, Joe!" were her exact words.

The entire weekend I thought about what I had heard. What had I gotten myself into?!? I wondered if I could succeed. To this point in my life, I had taken my business degree and self-confidence and succeeded in many challenges with no prior experience: as an Air Force administrative officer, as a business manager in several different businesses, as a teacher, a newspaper production supervisor, a real estate broker, and an assistant principal. Would being principal of Fenton be my Waterloo?

Fenton is hard to find without directions. After being lost for a half-hour, I finally arrived at my new school. My briefing at the region office never included any information about the actual school site itself, so I was pleasantly surprised by the campus: a square city block with multiple bungalow-type classrooms and more than seventy mature trees. Although desperately in need of maintenance, it appeared to be a "good-looking" school. Originally built to house 350 students, it now had 950.

My indoctrination at the region office was not exaggerated. If anything, they had softened the blow! It was certainly going to be the greatest challenge of my adult life! Undaunted by the teachers and parents who would brush me off with "I'll talk to you if you're still here in six months," I spent the next two years smiling, shaking hands, putting out "fires" everywhere, and eliminating the incredible number of inequities that permeated the organization. One thing I discovered was that all African American teacher assistants had six-hour positions while all Hispanic TAs had only three-hour assignments, although 60 percent of the students were Spanish-speaking Hispanics.

We made the campus safe and secure by adding gates, fencing, and lights. We reroofed and painted the entire school. The long line of staff who wanted to leave Fenton were shown the door. With no volunteer replacements, anyone who appeared willing to accept the challenge of working at Fenton was hired. At least they were willing to be there! For the first two years, I did not have an assistant principal. When one was assigned in 1990, it was like receiving reinforcements in battle!

"I assumed charter schools were just another paper reform movement. . . . Then I heard. . . that although the school district got $4,100 per student from the state, less than $2,900 reached our schools."

In 1991, a slumping economy, LAUSD's shortsightedness and the teachers' union practice of putting children second resulted in a 10 percent pay cut for all LAUSD employees. Other changes increased the norm for assistant principals. This resulted in a domino-effect bumping of personnel.

Fenton's assistant principal was bumped back to a coordinator's position and a new AP was assigned. I was not pleased! This action, however, has had the greatest positive impact on my professional life and on the lives of the members of the Fenton community. Our new AP, Irene Sumida, proved to be the shot in the arm we all needed; brilliant, caring unparalleled in instructional knowledge and ability, organized, goal-oriented, hard-working, unflappable, and a wonderful human being! Working side by side we accomplished much. It just wasn't enough!

Although Fenton was hardly the "hellhole" of five years ago, there were some undeniable facts:

- We were not impacting student achievement; standardized test scores were still in the single digits.
- Staff morale was low after the pay cut and years of "having things done to you."
- Most of our leadership team had made the decision to leave the district or even the state.
- My hands were raw from being slapped by those above me each time I circumvented the system to get something accomplished.

We were a group of educators who wanted to make a difference but were very close to abandoning Fenton, and I did not think I could handle another five years as an LAUSD principal in order to reach early retirement. Bearing all the responsibility but without any authority to make substantive changes was no way to manage. Our monthly principals' meetings had degenerated into "bitch sessions with lunch."

Dr. Yvonne Chan, a fellow principal, had been talking about her school leaving the district and becoming a charter school. I assumed charter schools were just another paper reform movement akin to moving the deck chairs around on the *Titanic*. Then I heard from our representative to a negotiating team that although the school district got $4,100 per student from the state, less than $2,900 reached our schools. I began listening to Yvonne and investigating the charter school concept.

I firmly believed that control of the decision-making process was not enough. You had to have control of the money and enough to make substantive changes. Yvonne and I teamed up and began asking questions about the money. Surprisingly, we could not get firm numbers from anyone we queried at the state and local levels. We ended up wading through LAUSD's prior year's financial statements—all three inches! We, too, were unable to extrapolate firm numbers. We were able to identify a range. We believed our students would generate between $4,300 and $4,800 each. Armed with this information, Yvonne and I went back to our schools and pushed on.

I costed out our current operation to determine current expenditure levels by LAUSD. I then created on paper "Joe's Dream School"; reducing class size from thirty-two to twenty-five, six additional teachers, a full-time counselor and psychologist, a full-time Family Center director, new textbooks, reversal of the pay cut. When I costed out my "Dream School," much to my surprise, I found that it was fiscally doable at the lower number of $4,300 per student.

Armed with this information, I began discussing converting to a charter school with our leadership team. We explored the concept daily for about ten days. With one exception, we agreed we would all stay at Fenton if we could become a charter school. (The one exception had already signed a contract with a district in Maryland, where he taught for one year, only to return to Fenton as our dean of students.)

We presented the idea to the staff at a faculty meeting and suggested they think about it. For two weeks, teachers met in small and large groups at various times throughout the day. We occasionally reassembled as a staff to ask questions and share ideas. At the end of the two weeks, over 95 percent of our teachers voted to commence writing a charter. California's Charter School Law at that time required that a charter be signed by 50 percent or more of the teachers at the school.

We divided into eleven writing teams and wrote our charter, attempting to create the perfect educational environment for the entire school community. We kept the few things that LAUSD did well, and we changed all the many things we disliked. We were going to empower a totally disenfranchised school community!

"The road to "charterdom" was a rocky one. . . . We fought it out on the front page of our local newspaper, in the board room, and at the negotiating table, and we utilized political and business allies . . . to get every cent our students deserved."

The road to "charterdom" was a rocky one. The state superintendent of schools interpreted the law that said "the State Superintendent of Public Instruction shall apportion the charter school entitlements" to mean that he would continue business as usual and let the sponsoring district give the charter schools their funds.

This set up an immediate adversarial relationship with the district. They were just attempting to create "paper" per-pupil budgets for schools who volunteered for their institutionalized reform efforts. They certainly didn't want to give charter schools more than their schools. Many uncomfortable situations arose. We fought it out on the front page of our local newspaper, in the board room, at the negotiating table, and we utilized political and business allies in an effort to get every cent our students deserved.

We could not begin operating on July 1, 1993, because LAUSD interpreted the sixty days they had by law to act on our charter as sixty working days. So we began operation as an independent charter school on January 1, 1994.

"We could no longer blame district staff, board rules, the union contract, or any outside entity for any condition that existed at our school."

It is truly amazing what can be accomplished when impediments—real or perceived—are eliminated. As a charter school, the finger-pointing ceased. We could no longer blame district staff, board rules, the union contract, or any outside entity for any condition that existed at our school. We were truly in charge of our destiny!

Attitudes changed, and so did behaviors. We were now both the employer and the employee. We underwent a metamorphosis. For example, schools are normally hotbeds for worker's compensation claims, and one Thursday morning, one of our kindergarten teachers fell in our parking lot and broke her ankle. She was a member of our Budget and Facilities Council. On Monday morning she was in a wheelchair teaching in her classroom. When I asked her why she was doing this, she replied, "I don't want our worker's compensation insurance rates to go up."

In 1997, ten years after I was assigned to the "hellhole," Fenton Avenue Charter School was named a California Distinguished School. We, however, were not finished. Success is a journey, not a destination. We accomplished much, but much is still to be done. The recent senseless deaths of two of our ex-students in a gang-related shooting but a half block from our school punctuate that charge.

Nonetheless, our accomplishments are quite incredible. Our students have demonstrated significant gains on performance indicators and standardized tests in each of the past nine years. Their educational environment is unparalleled at any elementary school anywhere. When visiting Fenton in 1996, state superintendent of Public Instruction Delaine Eastin stated, "I want to make sure education is a joy for every kid in California the way it is at Fenton Avenue Charter School." In June 1998, the most comprehensive case study of a charter school to date commissioned by LAUSD and conducted by WestEd concluded the following:

> "Relative to schools with similar demographic characteristics, Fenton has moved from the bottom to the top in rank in performance."

"The change in the school rank as compared to all other elementary schools with test data in the District . . . shows a large improvement . . . and an increase in rank."

"The data suggest strong evidence that the longer students stay at Fenton, the more likely they are to improve performance than students at comparison schools."

"We immediately recognized the idiocy of a principal as both instructional leader and business manager. Thus, we have co-directors."

Visitors from around the nation and several other countries ask, "What specifically are you doing differently?" My response is "everything!" First of all, we immediately recognized the idiocy of a principal as both instructional leader and business manager. Thus, we have co-directors. My partner, director of Instruction Irene Sumida, focuses on the most important function of the school while I concentrate on the financial management—bringing and sustaining resources to support instruction. We are in the most important business there is—the education of our youth. Nonetheless, it is a business and should be approached as such. When we expend our public dollars, we always try to get as much "cluck for the buck"—better, faster, cheaper.

As a school business, we must recruit outstanding teachers, or candidates who can be trained to be outstanding teachers. Without outstanding teachers, no school can be successful. To be most successful, even the best teacher needs the appropriate support and resources. Our teachers have the most sophisticated tools available. With a computer to student ratio of 1 to 1.5, our classrooms are the most technologically advanced of any elementary school anywhere in the world. This was achieved as the results of the leadership of a visionary teacher and is sustained through astute budgeting, business partners, multiyear contracts, and effective use of the E-Rate Program and the Qualified Zone Academy Bond Program.

As one of the largest public elementary charter schools in the nation (1,460, soon to be 1,600 when our current construction project is completed), we are faced with many challenges. As we deal with each, our guiding principle is: "Do what is in the best interest of our students." We help our students in many ways. Over 400 of them have computers at home, donated by business partners. Over 400 parents and community members are on campus each week, volunteering or learning themselves. Day and night adult literacy, ESL, citizenship, parenting, computer, and leadership classes are conducted in our Family Center. We also strive to work collaboratively as partners with all members of our school community. Everyone has a voice in what happens at our school.

Even our sponsoring district has been the recipient of our successes, though reluctantly. We have modeled true per-pupil budgeting, fee-for-service, and customer-oriented operations. We have generated millions of dollars in additional annual resources for them by demonstrating their way is not necessarily the best way.

What does it take to become a successful charter school? The Fenton Avenue Charter School experience would indicate the following:

- Strong and consistent leadership
- Outstanding teachers and staff
- Parents as partners
- Business and political partners
- A willingness to continually challenge the status quo
- Lots of hard work
- The development of internal instructional and business expertise
- A "can do" attitude
- Always putting children first

Chapter 6

Success Is a Journey, Not a Destination

Roughly fifteen years ago Joe Lucente wrote about his leadership adventure with the conversion of Fenton Avenue Elementary. His words "success is a journey, not a destination" hold true today. The journey continues.

Today, the leadership that transformed a failing school built in 1958 and converted it to Fenton Charter School in 1993 has now created a leadership organization that spans five schools rather than just the one. Based on the name of the original charter, this organization, called Fenton Charter Public Schools (FCPS), was created in 2011 and has grown from managing two schools (Fenton Charter and Fenton Primary Center), to directing the administration of five schools across the San Fernando Valley.

Unlike Vaughn, which grew linearly in the same geographic region to serve the same families and PK–12 students over time, Fenton has "grown" by helping other schools in the Los Angeles Unified School District (LAUSD), to achieve greater success through becoming charter schools. FCPS is now a CMO (charter management organization) for the five schools it currently manages and has a separate building with offices fulfilling the responsibilities of human resources, accounts payable, instructional technology, attendance, facilities and maintenance, and speciation education oversight. This business office serves all of the schools that they manage. Joe Lucente, as chairman of the board of directors, along with Irene Sumida, executive director, continues to be at the helm. What a journey!

Shared in their original story, at the time of its conversion, Fenton Avenue School was one of the two worst-performing schools in the region. (Vaughn was the other.) The school served 950 students (89% Hispanic, 8% African American, 65% English-language learner, 12% special needs, and 90% qualifying for free/reduced meals) in a high poverty area in Pacoima,

California. As principals of the traditional district schools Vaughn and Fenton, both Chan and Lucente saw the benefits of converting to charters, having more control over their journeys.

BROADENING THE SCOPE

Almost fifteen years following Fenton's conversion to charter status, in 2007 the Fenton Primary Center was opened across the street. This new primary center was a start-up charter (as opposed to a conversion charter such as Fenton) which was created to help move Fenton off of the year-round, multi-track calendar. It made possible the movement of the earlier grades from the original campus to the primary center. (In 2013, this primary center moved to its own 55,000 square foot site, less than a mile from Fenton Avenue Charter School.)

Meanwhile, LAUSD had made the decision to close a large school in East Hollywood that was not performing well. The director of that school came to Joe and Irene and asked if they could somehow partner with them to help out. Now with two schools (one conversion and one start-up), the Fenton leadership saw an opportunity to help more struggling schools in the valley such as this one, by creating the charter management organization.

FCPS was developed to ensure the long-term viability of the first two Fenton schools as well as to help others in the region. Seeing the tremendous success of Fenton Avenue Charter, the LAUSD agreed to let FCPS take on this additional failing school: Santa Monica Boulevard Community Charter School. The leadership accepted the challenge, and another larger conversion school was added to FCPS in 2012.

This nearly doubled the number of students FCPS was responsible for to 2,500. With three schools, FCPS continued to serve a demographic similar to the original conversion school to show what could be accomplished with poor students; these schools became among the highest performing schools with similar demographics in the area.

In August 2015, the two newest FCPS-managed schools were opened with 200 students each in kindergarten through fifth grade. These two schools, Fenton Charter Leadership Academy and the Fenton STEM Academy, are situated on one campus with a goal of maintaining a smaller population, housing a maximum of approximately 408 students in each school. Fenton Charter Leadership Academy focuses on social-emotional development to teach important social-emotional skills and create calm, confident, caring children. Fenton STEM Academy was developed to meet the needs of twenty-first-century learners with an emphasis on science and technology.

"His words, 'Success is a journey, not a destination' hold true today. The journey continues. Today, the leadership that transformed a failing school built in 1958, and converted it to Fenton Charter School in 1993, has now created a leadership organization that spans five schools rather than just the one."

At this point, the Fenton journey includes five schools with a staff of over 350 members serving over 3,000 students with an annual budget of almost $40 million, showing tremendous growth (and success) in a relatively short time.

Long after *Adventures of Charter School Creators* was written, Joe was asked about how Fenton was doing now; he was modest in his answer. "Obviously, much has changed at Fenton Avenue Charter School. No longer a single conversion charter school, the school is now part of a larger organization. A number of the administrative team members have come from our teaching staff, and a number of other employees have realized advancement within the organization. There truly is strength in numbers but also strength realized due to a reputation built over time. The relationship between our schools and our authorizing district is now positive, and the organization is thriving."

Back in 1987 when Joe Lucente had met with the LAUSD superintendent and administrators as their "last hope" to fix Fenton Avenue Elementary, a school that had been described as a "hellhole," who would have guessed that thirty years later, after converting to charter status, it would be celebrated as a model school? Fenton Avenue Charter School garnered many accolades along the journey since the conversion. It was recognized as a California Distinguished School in 1997 and received WASC and Cambridge Education accreditation in 2007.

Fenton is a certified member of the California Charter Schools Association and continues to be recognized as an example of one of the most successful conversion public charter schools in the nation. With a three-year average API of 809, in 2013 Fenton Avenue Charter School was recognized with the "Hart Vision Charter School of the Year Award" by the California Charter Schools Association (CCSA). The secret or not so secret ingredient to this organization's success is clearly due in large part to the passion and vision of its leaders, Joe Lucente and Irene Sumida.

VOICES FROM THE DREAM TEAM

As success is a journey and not a destination, the journey was begun by Joe but is now led by Irene Sumida, the sole executive director is FCPS, with the help of Joe who still serves as chair of the board of directors of the CMO. Bringing with her twenty-seven years of invaluable experience in LAUSD including having been an assistant principal, coordinator, classroom and mentor teacher, Irene and Joe made the perfect "dream team."

Although Joe had been a school principal prior to Fenton's conversion to charter status, his experience serving in the Air Force as well as his background degree in business administration was helpful. He had extensive experience managing some businesses and having a strong financial background gave him the confidence to handle the financial end of running a charter school. Irene's depth of experience in the classroom and as a prior school administrator complimented Joe's skills set.

During her eighteen years in the classroom, she was responsible for all state and federal compliance, and learned how to run the school as a substitute principal. She sat in on conferences with parents, ran meetings, oversaw programs, and was even responsible for student discipline. Irene described her experience, "It was excellent daily practice while continuing in the role I loved—teacher." The teacher and the businessman—although their skills sets are very different, their passion and work ethic are very much the same. Sharing their stories, each reminisced about the many hats they have worn and continue to wear from the custodian to construction project manager to public relations director!

"He had extensive experience managing some businesses and having a strong financial background gave him the confidence to handle the financial end of running a charter school. Irene's depth of experience in the classroom and as a prior school administrator complimented Joe's skills set."

Both Joe and Irene are humble when describing their roles in the school's accomplishments; however, each credits the other for much of the success. Joe credits Irene with the strong, successful leadership today. According to Joe, Irene maintains the forward movement and growth of Fenton through her outstanding relationships with district personnel and unbelievable strength of purpose. He adds, "She is the right person at the right time right now. She does the job of three people, and supposedly on a part time basis!" He commented on the dual leadership roles they have played and the evolution of that leadership over time:

> Vaughn and Fenton were the first two conversion charter schools in the country. So we were strange animals, no one knew how to handle us. And so it became a very interesting situation where we were butting heads with the district

consistently. And that is just the way my leadership had to be; that way at that point in time.

Today, for Irene, it's just the opposite. You know, because of our established success, because of our reputation, Fenton now is viewed as a very successful organization. And so now it's all about relationships. Irene has outstanding relationships with district personnel. And we can get things done that others can't.

When Irene speaks with passion about the school and its influence on the community, she gives much of the credit for her success to Joe. She stated, "Joe Lucente, who continued to be an advisor, friend and professional partner even after his 2005 retirement. . . . He was fearless, and he taught me courage—probably the most important characteristics necessary for effective and long-term charter leadership."

"Joe credits Irene with the strong, successful leadership today. According to Joe, Irene maintains the forward movement and growth of Fenton through her outstanding relationships with district personnel and unbelievable strength of purpose."

All of the charter leaders in this book were interviewed regarding their leadership styles. Joe shared the following story not found in the original *Adventures* book, but relevant to the type of charter leadership he exhibited:

Question: What characteristics/skills do you think your staff/teachers would use when describing your leadership?
Joe: I think that most would say that I'm pretty strong, that I'm caring, and that I'm trustworthy.
Question: Can you share an event or outcome that would reflect your leadership.
Joe: Yeah, I think probably the most telling would have been when we began to build the Fenton Primary Center. We had a 1.9 acre plot of land that had several buildings, horse stall, pool, septic tanks. It was quite a sight to actually clear. Our timeline was that we had to get this school built in 8 months in order to open by the following August. About four months in, it became evident to me that our development company, our contractor, and our architect were not going to deliver this on time based on what I was seeing. So I decided it was time for me to take some action. I just went in and because in California the way things are set up, we can get reimbursement for leases but we cannot get reimbursement for debt services. So the school is set up so we have an LLC, a Limited Liability Corporation that holds the property, and I am the president of that organization. So I can legitimately say that I am the owner. I went in and I started to

look to see what was going on and why things were slowing down and it was pretty obvious to me that the contractor was not managing the site the way I felt they should be. The people were standing around wasting time, etc. So I started roaming the site and when I found someone who was having a third break in an hour, I asked them if they planned to continue working there. They asked me, "Who in the blank are who?" And I said, "I'm the blanking owner, that's who. And if you want to continue working here, get to it or leave." So word got around, but I didn't feel like that was enough so for the next four months, I spent 8 to 10 hours a day on that site just roaming around making sure everything got done. And we did bring it in exactly 8 months. We opened a 50 thousand foot three story school for 820 students. And we did it for 15 million dollars.

Having lived and worked in both the charter world and the traditional school world, Joe shared another story depicting the sharp contrast, putting the building story into perspective:

I'll give you an example of what a feat that really is. I am on a board of YFX Charter School and we are building a school for 400, half the size of our primary center. But we are doing it on an LAUSD site so there's no land cost, but we have to do it according to LAUSD, use their specs, use their personnel, and of course, we have to follow the California Department of State Architecture Rules and Regulations for Schools. As a result, it is taking us four years to build this school and it is costing is 24 million dollars and we have no income yet because there are no students there.

When asked what characteristics and skills her staff might use in describing her leadership, Irene's approach was somewhat different, more instructional and community focused. She shared her thoughts through the following:

I have often told my staff that we must always conduct ourselves with the "*4 Rs*" in mind: always working to build *relationships*, *respect*, *reputation* and *resiliency*. During the past 22 years, I have built strong *relationships* with other charter leaders, with our authorizing district, with legislators and with our school community. *Respect* is key to building these relationships, which in turn builds a *reputation*. And finally, *resiliency*—never give up and work tenaciously to accomplish your goals.

While Joe and Irene are humble about their roles as leaders in the charter school world, their communities celebrate them with many accolades, through public recognition and awards. In 2012, Irene and Joe both received the Legacy Award at the 20th Annual Charter Schools Conference, an honor given to stewards of the charter school movement over the last twenty years.

Most recently in May of 2017, Irene was recognized as one of five "Women of the Year" honored by the Downtown Los Angeles Japanese American Citizen's League and Japanese Women's Society of Southern California.

"She stated, 'Joe Lucente, who continued to be an advisor, friend and professional partner even after his 2005 retirement. . . . He was fearless, and he taught me courage—probably the most important characteristics necessary for effective and long-term charter leadership.'"

THE FUTURE OF CHARTER SCHOOLS

All of the leaders in this book were also given an opportunity to share their thoughts on the future of the charter school movement and what kind of preparation might be needed for future charter leaders. When asked about the future of the charter school movement, Joe immediately commented on the business perspective:

> I think for a mom and pop type charter school, you know, just a one only school that wants to be started by a few parents or a few teachers, it is less attractive definitely. For a strong CMO that is successful, I would say it is close to a wash because there are many positive things that exist today that didn't twelve years but then there are also many negatives that you have to deal with. It just takes so much of a leader's time away from the important stuff. The positives are that there are vehicles today for financing facilities that didn't exist twelve years ago. There also is Prop 39 in Los Angeles, in California, which is helps small charter schools get located on a district site to get started. There are the federal grants. There are Walton grants here in California. There is money on the table that wasn't there before. It's just the atmosphere. The landscape has changed so drastically that you are under a constant microscope which, you know, that's a two-edged sword. You want to be accountable, but we don't want to spend all of our time meeting those accountability requirements.

Regarding advice for future charter leaders, he notes:

> I think what I've learned over the years is that you can't ever know enough. You need to learn as much as you possibly can. The more you learn the better off you are. I also feel that the best way to learn is by emulating a successful leader. So shadowing successful leaders is probably a strong way to develop future leaders.

And as I look around, and I see in that leadership, in a lot of charter schools today, I do not see a lot of really strong new leaders, and I think that if we are going to be successful, successful charter school leaders must develop future charter school leaders. It's something that will accelerate or slow down future successful charter schools. So in our organization, we spend a great deal of time fostering leadership, because we want to develop strong leaders and have people step up and learn. There is a very, what I call, telling difference between my generation, Irene's generation, and the generation of those now who are stepping into leadership. We, however, always felt that there was no task that was below us. We just rolled up our sleeves and did what had to get done. Today I see a lot of these younger people going into leadership; they are the types that want a 9-to-5 job. You know, they are more interested in being looked to as a leader, but not always willing to roll up their sleeves and show others, you know, that they can do it, too.

Question: And how to do you think that we can effectively deal with that situation?

Joe: I think that we have to point out to our leaders that if they want to be respected and if they want to be really effective leaders, they have to show the people on their staff that they are will to do anything to help the school move forward. And if that means picking up a broom at a certain time, then do it. Nothing should be beneath them. They should be willing to roll up their sleeves and do whatever has to get done in order to move the school forward.

Irene took more of an instructional leader approach to the questions:

As the charter movement has grown, there is even greater scrutiny of every aspect of charter school management. Running a charter school is very much like running a school district, just on a smaller scale, and—with far fewer resources. Today's charter leader must be knowledgeable about curriculum, instruction, federal and state laws, employment practices, school finance, and state and federal legislation. They must have the ability to speak to and for their school communities, build relationships amongst all stakeholders, and seek and garner every possible resource for their schools. I believe that those seeking to improve public education will always view the charter school movement as an enticing route.

An administrative credential program is very helpful, but even if focused on charter school leadership, it will provide only basic knowledge about the day-to-day decisions leaders must make. Most importantly, I would encourage everyone to take considerable time to hone his/her teaching skills and instructional experience, and not be in a hurry to leave the classroom. There is much to be learned about running a school effectively, any school, from the perspective of the classroom teacher.

One clear lesson learned from both Fenton Charter Public Schools and Vaughn Next Century Learning Center is that it sometimes takes years of dedication, perseverance, hard work, and the ability and willingness to change or grow when needed to cultivate successful schools. The work, over time, appears much like parenting; roles change as the child (or school) develops over time.

Irene's advice for future charter school leaders shares similarities with advice one might share with a new parent, "Charter leaders need to focus more on the uncertainties that exist in the charter world, emphasizing that leaders must be ready for everything and anything that may be encountered." She continued, "This includes potentially disastrous state and federal legislation; changes in the politics of the state, which may affect funding and regulations; and the need to be continually engaged with the authorizing district. Charter leaders need to know the reality of the work they will begin and walk into the role with 'eyes wide open.' The role requires a level of commitment, dedication, hard work, and even sacrifices that many cannot imagine, and they must love what they do."

The journey is long. The children and their schools grow and develop along many varied continuums that interweave through the years and affect different strands and educators must adapt. Our attempts to separate them out over time into social ("that's the community's job") or emotional ("that's the parent's role") do not lend themselves to establishing optimum environments in which to raise our children.

For healthy development, the whole child should be considered and that environment, particularly the learning environment, includes a caring, sustained relationship with adults who care deeply about the students over time. These two conversion charters accomplished this. At Fenton, "Over 400 parents and community members are on campus each week, volunteering or learning themselves. Day and night adult literacy, ESL, citizenship, parenting, computer, and leadership classes are conducted in our Family Center" (see chapter 5 of this book).

If either the parents or school community is unresponsive or just unavailable in any one capacity, the children's academic achievement and future may be compromised. Fenton Charter Public Schools and Vaughn Next Century Learning Center both lead as partners with their communities to see that individual needs are met, and their successes are evident and celebrated throughout their communities.

This level of dedication to the community found at both Fenton and Vaughn may be well beyond what is typically seen in many traditional school districts. Traditional school leaders generally come and go, are transferred from school to school, or leave of their own accord perhaps for higher salaries or to move up a district hierarchy, thus missing the important relationship-building opportunities needed for some students to achieve success. Class sizes in some schools can be so large that teachers barely know the names of their students.

Joe and Irene and Yvonne and Anita appear to understand the need for a personalized environment for students to thrive. Both Fenton's and Vaughn's leaders remained working for the school in some capacity, often modifying their leadership roles to best serve the community at the time and over time. Though Joe technically retired in 2005, he remains an important part of the "dream team" as the chair of the Board of Fenton Charter Public Schools. Irene attempted to retire in 2010; however, she worked unpaid for that year and returned at the board's request the next year. "Commitment, dedication, hard work, and sacrifice!"

"One clear lesson learned from both Fenton Charter Public Schools and Vaughn Next Century Learning Center is that it sometimes takes years of dedication, perseverance, hard work, and the ability and willingness to change or grow when needed to cultivate successful schools. The work, over time, appears much like parenting; roles change as the child (or school) develops over time."

Like Yvonne and Anita, both Joe and Irene have served in many leadership capacities at the organizations they created (founder, co-leaders, executive directors, board of directors, even unpaid project construction managers) for an almost fifty years combined effort. Both pairs of leaders are focused on the future of their learning communities as they make a succession plan for their departure.

As Joe and Irene look toward that future, Irene shared her thoughts on her own journey, "In terms of leading a charter school, I must say that the charter world was so new and uncharted that Joe and I simply focused on what we could do to create the perfect school. For me, it was about creating the school I would have wanted for my own children; the school where I would have wanted to work as a teacher; and the place all parents would gladly enroll their children." And as Anita reminds us, "This is most definitely a Labor of Love."

Chapter 7

A District School

Feaster-Edison Charter School

By Libia S. Gil, Lowell Billings, Ana Tilton, Rick Werlin, and Dennis Doyle

BACKGROUND BY LIBIA S. GIL

Dr. Libia S. Gil was appointed to the superintendency of the Chula Vista Elementary School District in August 1993. During her tenure, the district has experienced continuous growth and is currently serving more than 24,000 students in 39 schools. Gil has fostered the successful implementation of numerous school change models including five charter schools and partnerships with Edison Schools Inc., School Futures Research Foundation, Accelerated Schools, Comer, Standards-Based Instruction, and the Ball Foundation. In 1998, the community passed a $95 million school bond with a 76 percent voters' approval to support modernization of learning environments. Gil began her teaching career in the Los Angeles Unified School District and has taught in various programs, including English as a Second Language and Gifted and Talented programs. During her teaching experiences, she and her colleagues created a successful K–12 alternative school and numerous alternative classroom programs.

Chris Whittle was one of the keynote presenters at California's statewide Superintendents' Symposium in January 1996. This was the pivotal event that provided the exposure to the Edison Project, which grabbed my immediate attention and desire to learn more. Within a week, I was corresponding with Chris Whittle to exchange information about our school district and the Edison Project goals and timelines.

The following month I contacted all principals to determine if their schools had any interest in exploring a potential partnership with the Edison Project. To our surprise, eleven out of the thirty-three principals responded affirmatively. Additional Edison program materials and project overviews were distributed to all interested principals.

In May 1996, Bill Kirby, former Texas State Education commissioner representing Edison, met with a group of interested principals. Due to conflicting schedules, actual participants in this session represented six schools. There was high receptivity and enthusiasm for the Edison program design, with the emphasis on restructuring instructional time, reorganizing school governance, and providing a comprehensive curriculum in each content area supported by intensive staff development. With the addition of technology as a teaching-learning tool, the focus on improving student achievement was most appealing. The enthusiasm dampened when the topic of reconstituting staff, including the principal, was presented. Although most principals readily welcomed the opportunity to select staff members, they found it difficult to apply the process to themselves.

In the next several months, discussions continued among principals and with executive Edison staff members. In August 1996, we formally contacted the teachers' union and the classified employee organization to inform them about a board presentation by Chris Whittle, who provided an overview of the Edison Project that highlighted the conceptual framework for supporting student achievement. All of our board members were intrigued with the Edison model and responded positively to our continued exploration.

In September 1996, several planning sessions between executive administrators from both organizations occurred. Questions on potential school site options, financial parameters, development of support, and overall timetable were addressed. It was quickly determined that a schoolwide Title I qualified school would be most desirable to create the necessary economies of scale in addition to the need for improving student performance.

Seven schoolwide Title I schools were identified as potential partnership options. Subsequently, nine principals of Title I schools were contacted to determine interest level. In this round, two principals expressed a definite interest. Edison staff visited the interested school sites and met with each principal to discuss the Edison concept and implications for implementation.

"Ironically, parent and student feedback rated the school and teachers positively, in contrast to teachers' rating parents and students poorly."

To support a successful Edison Project implementation in California, Chris Whittle created the three-legged partnership model to include philanthropic entities for start-up capital. Numerous regional donors were contacted, and initial expanded facilities and technology investments were supported by major donations to the project.

SCHOOL SELECTION

By October, the Feaster principal remained the only one with serious interest in exploring the Edison project. Simultaneously, Feaster was considering school change vehicles to address the dismal pattern of student achievement, unruly student behavior, poor attendance, negative school climate, and one of the worst school reputations in the region. All common school data, including customer satisfaction survey results, indicated a low-performing school with low staff morale and low expectations for students.

Ironically, parent and student feedback rated the school and teachers positively, in contrast to teachers' rating parents and students poorly. The discrepancy in attitudes demanded strong interventions to raise the level of expectations for student learning in a community that had accepted school failure as the norm.

Dialogue participants expanded and continued at multiple levels of the organization, including Feaster school staff, parents, district administration, and Edison staff members. In November 1996, a representative team composed of the Feaster principal, teacher, parent, two school board members, and I visited an established Edison Project school in Colorado Springs. The teachers' union president decided to join us at the last minute. The observations and interactions with students, parents, and teachers reinforced our interest and created greater excitement to pursue a potential Edison partnership. The Feaster school representatives returned to their school community with renewed energy and spirit.

The positive energy and hope for a new future at Feaster school was quickly challenged by the teachers' union, whose leadership attempted to sabotage the interest. It was not unusual to have a parent meeting disrupted with charges that all staff would be fired and other unfounded allegations to derail support for the Edison Project.

FEASTER-EDISON CHARTER

In January 1997, a team of representative teachers and principal, Dr. Catherine Rodriguez, toured one of the original Edison Schools in Wichita, Kansas. They wanted to observe firsthand the program implementation process and impact on students, parents, and staff. The outcome of this visit solidified the team interest and commitment to pursue the Edison model. They were all impressed and convinced that the program design provided a high potential to maximize student learning.

"Despite the regular ongoing discussions with the local teachers' union leaders . . . they continued to bombard individual staff members with misinformation and intimidation tactics."

Despite the regular ongoing discussions with the local teachers' union leaders and daily responses to inquiries regarding a possible conversion to a charter, the union leaders continued to bombard individual staff members with misinformation and intimidation tactics. Tenured teachers were understandably nervous to hear that they would lose many rights, including seniority and tenure status in the school district.

They were also concerned that they could be terminated at any time in a charter school without due process and would have no right to return to the school district. Although charter legislation already provides job protection for teachers who do not wish to teach at a charter school, we responded immediately with board action to reinforce that "any Feaster teacher who does not want to be part of the program will be guaranteed a teaching position in the district."

This action contradicted all the misconceptions of teacher status perpetuated by the local union; however, it served to intensify their local, state, and national propaganda distribution to staff and community to raise public opposition. The issue now focused on the lack of inclusion in the process and anti-privatization sentiments. Fortunately, all segments of the community had been included in a proactive communication plan: I had personally met with elected officials, including the mayor, members of the CV Chamber of Commerce board, Council of PTAs, District Parent Advisory Committee members, other community leaders, and the press corps.

On March 4, 1997, the Chula Vista Elementary School Board unanimously approved the Feaster staff charter school petition supported by over two-thirds of the teaching staff despite teacher union allegations of improprieties with the voting process. On March 13, 1997, a representative team of a parent, a teacher, Edison staff, district staff, and I went to Sacramento to witness the California State Board of Education approve the Feaster-Edison Charter School petition.

Prior to that meeting, I had contacted and lobbied every state board member for their support on the petition. It was not official: the first Edison charter school partnership in the state. We felt the joyous culmination of many months of effort to create a new school model for our students, as well as a new beginning with renewed staff and community enthusiasm and dedication to increase student achievement.

PUBLIC/PRIVATE PARTNERSHIP: A BUSINESS PERSPECTIVE, BY LOWELL BILLINGS

Dr. Lowell Billings has spent twenty-six years in public education as a K–6 teacher, principal of West View School, and director of research and technology in the South Bay Union School District. In 1991, he was appointed assistant superintendent for instructional services and is currently the assistant superintendent for business services for the Chula Vista Elementary School District. He serves as chief financial officer, chief planner for school construction/renovation, and director of district operational support services.

Feaster Elementary School had a long and well-documented history of providing substandard educational programs. By any measure, its success with students was well below Chula Vista Elementary School District and state standards. Consistently, Feaster was the poorest-performing district school. When Feaster became a charter school, a number of staff left, which provided flexibility to reinvent expectations and standards for instruction. Simultaneously, class size reduction was implemented, which brought one new staff member for every two teachers in grades K–3.

At the same time, over $3 million in modernization renovation and repair was completed. Additionally, four acres of adjacent property were acquired to augment what was one of the smallest school sites in the district. The resulting partnership with Edison brought over $800,000 of capital funds to provide classrooms for the rapidly growing student population in this sector of the district.

> **"When Feaster became a charter school, a number of staff left, which provided flexibility to reinvent expectations and standards for instruction."**

These circumstances proved beneficial for start-up of the project partnership. California per-pupil funding was marginal for the program-rich Edison. The large size of the school was countered through creation of school-within-a-school houses, which reduced the size of the school to more manageable components.

Creation of a fiscally independent public/private for-profit venture was daunting. Support for this model, although unanimously supported by the local governing board, was not routinely embraced by various state agencies. The State Teachers' Retirement System, the Public Employees' Retirement System, the San Diego County Joint Powers Authority Insurance/Liability consortium, and the San Diego Joint County Office of Education all questioned the fit with our public education charge. Chula Vista Elementary School District's standard reply was that public education constitutes a multimillion-dollar for-profit business opportunity.

Textbooks, insurance, construction contracts, software, computer hardware, furniture, and equipment have long provided for-profit opportunities. The Edison Project merely requested equal business opportunity, only this time for direct services in a teaching and learning delivery model.

Formation of a public/private for-profit partnership threatened the existence of established institutions, roles, functions, and areas of real or perceived jurisdiction. Nowhere was this clearer than with the teachers' association. Elements of the charter such as merit pay, differentiated teacher job descriptions, extended school day/year, and charter precedence over union contracts, coupled with the voluntary flight of some senior teachers, were some of the impacts and effects that the union viewed as negative and threatening.

It's interesting to note that the classified union, through an interest-based approach, found the charter and the public/private for-profit partnership to be a new and unique opportunity for students in the school. Under this arrangement, issues were openly discussed and resolved.

"Formation of a public/private for-profit partnership threatened the existence of established institutions, roles, functions, and areas of real or perceived jurisdiction."

Edison staff worked very hard to involve both classified and certificated bargaining units while developing charter language. This effort was undertaken to create buy-in and support. The teachers' union efforts to disrupt the process and waylay the charter were ultimately unsuccessful.

Due to the complexity of the Edison partnership design, there was a need for a solid fiscal independence model with clear operational structure that defined district and charter roles and responsibilities. Great efforts were made to develop this foundation document, which later served as a template for numerous other charters within and outside the district. This afforded the district opportunity to reflect on its service and support model as cost centers were defined and quantified. Value added became a key definition for support.

REFORM EFFORTS, BY ANA TILTON

Ana Tilton is a senior vice president of the School Division for Edison Schools Inc., the largest educational management company in the United States. She oversees all school operations for the Western Division of the company, encompassing approximately 65 schools in 8 states, with an enrollment of approximately 40,000 students. Prior to joining Edison in 1999, she had a long career as a California public school administrator; she served as superintendent of the Soquel School District, assistant superintendent for the Chula Vista School District, and principal in the Carlsbad Unified School District.

I love a simple story with a profound message. One of my favorite children's books is *The Little Engine That Could*. You know the one: "I think I can, I think I can, I think I can." As a teacher, I thrilled at the chorus reading and discussion that followed from all ages regarding the little engine that saved the day for all the children on the other side of the mountain. As you may guess, I am also the eternal optimist when it comes to providing a world-class education for *all* children.

In 1995 and 1996, as a cabinet member in the Chula Vista Elementary School District, I coached a school in crises. Feaster Elementary School students continually scored at the bottom on all indicators of success: attendance, norm-referenced testing, district criterion-referenced assessment, community involvement, and mobility. Teacher morale was low, students did not display pride in work or self, excuses were made for low performance, and schoolwide decisions were not made based on student needs but on adult wants.

It was clear to district leadership that this was a *Little Engine That Could* in need of a shove to start the journey in reaching "our shared vision." One of the sentences in the district's vision statement reads: "The entire educational community accepts the challenge of change and is motivated to acquire skills and values for a rapidly changing world." Both the superintendent and the entire school board embraced change and sought out partnerships in creating a challenging educational experience for all children. Through an inclusive effort, Feaster joined other schools in examining different reform efforts.

Edison School design is highly ambitious, encouraging fundamental change in school structure. They offer a longer school day, longer school year, rich and challenging curriculum for all students, extensive professional development for teachers and administrators, technology for an information age, and careful assessment that provides accountability. In partnership with the district reform efforts, Edison Schools offered a new vision of the future.

In August 1997, Feaster-Edison Charter School opened its doors to students and families. This was only the beginning of a five-year journey to dramatic reform on behalf of children. This little engine not only had a heavy load to take up the hill but also had people blocking the tracks. Despite the obstacles, Feaster-Edison Charter School is on the other side of the hill and delivering on its promise to children. In the fifth year of design implementation, it has demonstrated steady and significant growth in student achievement evidence by multiple measures.

This story of success is not over. The staff and community are looking for new mountains to climb and are not satisfied with the great gains. They want to continue their reform efforts and increase the gains for all children. I am proud to say I was part of this story. I have since left the district to become a superintendent and now work for Edison Schools overseeing the operations of thirty Edison School partnerships across the nation.

FEAR OR FACT, BY RICK WERLIN

Rick Werlin received his bachelor's degree in elementary education from the State University of New York and master's degree in educational administration from Texas Southern University in Houston. He has served as a special education, bilingual, and general education elementary teacher. His instructional leadership experiences include elementary assistant principal and principal, middle school principal, and alternative high school principal. He has worked in human resources in three major districts in Texas and has served as the assistant superintendent for human resources services and support for Chula Vista for the past five years.

"Watch out, you're going to lose all your benefits." "There go all your teacher rights out the door." These were all too familiar comments made to teachers at Feaster-Edison Charter School when they were trying to make a decision on collective bargaining per the Migden Bill (AB 631), which required all California charter schools to make a decision by March 31, 2000, as to whether they were going to declare themselves or the school district the "employer for collective bargaining purposes." The latter would automatically allow for the sole representative, Chula Vista Educators, part of the California Teachers Association and NEA, to represent them and have a closed shop.

Teachers at Feaster-Edison voted not to declare their charter school as the "employer for collective bargaining purposes," therefore disassociating themselves from the teachers' union. The union not only lost approximately $800 annual dues from almost eighty teachers but faced the shocking reality that all five of our district charter schools had elected the same path.

Rather than choosing the path of fear and deception, district representatives provided factual information so that teachers would be well informed prior to their election of their options. This district approach is directly related to our core belief that it is our responsibility to empower our staff with the tools and knowledge to better provide students options for success.

THEN AND NOW, BY DENNIS DOYLE

Since 1997, Dennis M. Doyle has served as an assistant superintendent in the Chula Vista Elementary School District, the largest K–6 district in California. Prior to accepting his current position, he was director of educational partnerships for Lightspan, Inc., a multimedia educational technology company. Previously, he worked as an administrator for eight years in the San Diego Unified School District.

Francisco Escobedo, Feaster-Edison principal, showcased the data to the Chula Vista Elementary School District Board of Education in June 2003. Feaster-Edison Charter School was making the school's annual presentation to the board, a requirement assumed by all charter schools. Prior to the Edison conversion, Francisco explained, Feaster's enrollment consisted of 781 students. Six years later the school had grown to 1,137 pupils. Students who routinely left their neighborhood school for spaces in other district schools had all come home. There was space at the local school, programs were exciting and appealing, and all neighborhood students could be accommodated.

The student population, Francisco noted, had become more Hispanic over that period of time, growing from 72 percent to 80 percent Latino. The percentage of Feaster-Edison students who were limited-English proficient/English language learners climbed just slightly, from 50 percent to 54 percent. The population is poorer than it was before Feaster became an Edison School; the percentage of students qualifying for free or reduced-price lunch grew from 74 percent to 100 percent. Of particular interest was the change in mobility rates. Edison data show declines sharply from 58 percent in 1996–1997 to 19 percent in 2002–2003. With additional facilities, Feaster-Edison was becoming a more stable learning environment over time. Attendance showed demonstrable improvement as well, with reductions in absenteeism every year in succession.

"Data (on mobility rates) show declines sharply from 58 percent . . . to 19 percent (four years later)."

By every measure, academic achievement was up. More students were reading at grade level (6% in 1997, 72% in 2003). The number of bilingual students who began English reading on an annual basis had grown steadily as well.

What Francisco did not know was that new standardized test scores had just been released and the spring reading schools had risen dramatically from the baseline year. Indeed, graduating sixth graders saw their cohort Normal

Curve Equivalent (NCE) scores grow from 30.0 as second graders in 1997–1998 to 42.0 NCE in 2002–2003, a 12.0 NCE change. Math scores, too, had risen to new heights.

The same graduating sixth graders showed cohort gains from 30.0 NCE in 1997–1998 in second grade to 48.3 NCE last year, an 18.3 NCE improvement. Language scores grew for the cohort from 27.0 NCE as 1997–1998's second graders to 49.8 NCE last year (22.8 NCE change). Spelling improved from 31.0 NCE to 43.7 NCE (a 12.5 NCE net gain) for the cohort over the five years. More students than ever before were meeting district standards, as measured by a set of conjunctive multiple measures. Just 37.76 percent of students met district reading/language arts and math standards in 1997–1998, rising to 44.23 percent last year.

Student, staff, and parent ratings of the school as measured by the prestigious Harris Interactive Survey have soared. For example, before Edison, 68 percent of parents graded the school as "A" or "B" for atmosphere. In the last rating, 82 percent graded Feaster-Edison an "A" or "B." In the recent student-led Quarterly Learning conferences, 98 percent of parents attended.

"There were parents with tears in their eyes, grateful for the transformation."

Earlier in the month, Francisco met with parent members of the Feaster-Edison Charter School community. Over 159 parents attended. There were parents with tears in their eyes, grateful for the transformation Edison had provided. It was a very emotional meeting. The principal reported that the idea of an Edison Middle School Academy was brought up. Parents, Francisco stated emphatically, love the Edison model.

For students, there have been other major changes. For example, once staff discovered through data analysis that twenty students accounted for 73 percent of disciplinary referrals, it took just five months' implementation of a resiliency mentoring program (each student was adopted by one staff member) to reduce referrals for those twenty students to just 28 percent.

SYSTEMIC CHANGE, BY LIBIA S. GIL

We have supported and encouraged charter schools in our district based on some of the following assumptions:

- Belief in providing options and alternative pathways to improve student learning. We are committed to high expectations, common standards,

and accountability goals for student achievement, but we do not subscribe to a single model or program to meet the unique needs of all children.
- Belief that increased flexibility at the school level provides increased opportunities for ownership and responsibility for student learning outcomes. This is a natural extension of a highly decentralized approach to our district operations.
- Belief that charter schools provide a strong vehicle with the potential to not only transform student learning at their particular site but also to impact the entire educational system.

What impact has Feaster-Edison Charter School made on the district? Debunking the myths that for-profit privatization is inherently evil and that we had betrayed the public education system was the first attitudinal challenge we had to address districtwide with skeptics and resisters to change. The most common questions are as follows:

Why for profit? Why allow them to make money off our children? We can point to the myriad of equipment, services, textbooks, other materials, facilities, technology, and so on, that the public school system currently purchases from private vendors who are profit making.

Why have you given up on public schools? Our best response is quite the contrary: we are strengthening our public schools because we will not give up on our children!

What can they do that we can't do ourselves? Our response is: We can write our own curriculum, train our teachers, extend the school year, and do our own research, but how long would it take to accomplish what Edison has already completed with their investment of time and resources in research and development?

Other general impacts include the following:

- The process for creating a charter proposal is a model for building a unity of purpose with staff and community engagement.
- We challenged the status-quo thinking and stimulated new practices to open minds to other possibilities for service delivery models. A major attitudinal shift occurs from "can't do" to "can do" that permeates all levels of the system. From a traditional public school principal's perspective: The charter school movement has opened doors for traditional public schools. Many of the innovations used by the charter schools are applicable within the confines of a traditional bureaucracy. Processes include program planning,

peer coaching, differentiated staffing, extended day programs, etc. Charter schools have modeled possibilities for other school change efforts.
- One of the most significant impacts is raising the expectation and demand for responsive customer-service orientation from the central office. For example, when the first charter school contracted with a private landscaper, our district landscaping crew was stunned and dismayed. They quickly learned what value-added service and customer satisfaction meant. You can be assured that they started immediately removing all grass cuttings instead of piling them where children can trip on them and avoided mowing outside a classroom during instructional time, and they certainly improved their response time to staff requests at every school.
- Establishing accountability has raised expectations for all schools and refocused the entire system outcomes and results.
- Efficiency concerns and cost-effective practices caused the analysis of cost centers for services and goods.
- The expectations for performance outcomes were raised and aligned with appropriate compensation based on merit system rather than longevity.
- Ultimately, the greatest impact area was collective bargaining. The fact that all charter school's staffs voted to disassociate themselves from the local teachers' union sent a clear message that teachers value flexibility and do not want to be constrained by a collective bargaining agreement that demands uniformity. Some of the practices in charter school, such as a differentiated pay structure, teacher peer evaluations, home visits, and calendar and schedule changes, would be difficult if not impossible to implement under current collective bargaining agreement and philosophical differences.

There is no question that charter schools, and in particular Feaster-Edison, have made an impact on the traditional public schools in the Chula Vista Elementary School District. The question for us going forward is how do we determine the significance of impact on student learning?

Chapter 8

Strengthening Unlikely Partnerships

A School District, a District Charter, and Their Community

When this journey began, Francisco Escobedo led Feaster-Edison Charter School as its principal. He was the one principal who had the courage and initiative to see the potential of forming a partnership. Escobedo sought to change the persistent low performance of Feaster Elementary School. He believed he could positively affect the outcome, and he did. The partnership created the conversion charter school, Feaster-Edison Charter School, and it became a part of a public/private for-profit partnership with Edison management.

A major proponent of the partnership was then the district superintendent, Libia S. Gil, who saw an opportunity to improve one of the lowest performing schools in the district. Today, Escobedo, the founding principal of Feaster Charter, is the district superintendent of the Chula Vista Elementary School District, the district that houses the Feaster Charter School. Feaster's current executive director is Francisco Velasco who has been executive director of the school since 2002. The school has grown, adding a middle school, new twenty-first-century curriculum, and two additional principals. Edison is no longer in partnership with the school.

PARTNERSHIPS WITHIN THE DISTRICT

Still very connected to the charter world, Francisco Escobedo oversees seven charters: five dependent charters, and two independent charters that are part of the district. Five are conversion charters. He is also a professor at San Diego State University, and teaches a course for charter school principals. This district and its charters seem to have followed the original intentions of the development of charter schools, districts and charter schools sharing the responsibility of providing the best education for children. How has Escobedo wed the charter world within the traditional world of school districts?

Chula Vista Elementary School District, the state's largest elementary district, is located just 7.5 miles from downtown San Diego and 7.5 miles from the Mexican border in the South Bay area of southern California. With forty-eight schools (including the seven charters), the district's population is nearly 70 percent Hispanic, 13 percent white, 11 percent Filipino, and 7 percent African American or Asian/Pacific Islander. Escobedo's philosophy seems to have remained the same as his philosophy when leading his charter years ago; he believes in continuous improvement, and not resting on the district's laurels.

With an impressive list of accolades and awards for academic success received by Chula Vista Elementary School District, Escobedo is not complacent. He forms partnerships with local organizations that push the district forward to best serve its children and families.

"This district and its charters seem to have followed the original intentions of the development of charter schools, districts and charter schools sharing the responsibility of providing the best education for children."

COMMUNITY PARTNERSHIPS

Just as he was integral in forming the partnership with Edison many years before, he continues to partner with organizations that can elevate the district toward its research-based goals. One such initiative is the library card project. The library card project is part of a partnership with the Chula Vista Public Library to get more children to achieve reading proficiency by third grade by giving more than 7,000 free library cards to all kindergarten and first grade students. Improving academic success is not the only area where Escobedo leads with purpose. When asked to talk about an event or outcome that would reflect his leadership, Escobedo shared his response to the issue of obesity in schools:

> Back in 2010, I embarked with a mission of improving the total health footprint of our district. We have a significant number of students that we were able to calculate that they were obese level. We conducted a test where we measured the BMI of 25,000 students, and the results were pretty sobering.

And so, one of the things that I did was brought in many partners: parents, the Heart Association, hospitals nearby, and leaders as well. We really changed our culture and how to enhance our life styles, changed our life styles by healthy eating, improved exercise, and monitoring important vitals.

In the time of awareness that changed our culture and the school, we had families improve their health point tremendously. In fact the last five years, we had a 70 percent reduction of obesity level. And we have a great number of kids that are in the normal weight range, and we were able to move really a significant number of over a 1,000 students from a pre-diabetic stage to a stage where they could live a normal life.

So, as a result we got numerous recognitions. The most recent one, we won the California Golden Bell Award for our wellness focus in the state of California.[1]

Relying on current research to inform best practices and forming partnerships to solve the issues facing his students and families has brought success to the district which may be a key component in the success of partnering charter schools within the Chula Vista district. As Escobedo discussed the potential of charter schools development, he discussed the importance of an environment where there is dialogue among leaders:

I think you have to have the right setting; the right environment. You have to create an environment where there is dialogue between leaders, and you can be very successful. In fact, in our district, people visit our charter schools to see how they do things differently, and then we try to adapt some of those changes within a traditional setting. Unless there are structures that allow or enable that dialogue or that discourse to occur then we are working in isolation, and there will not be any growth.[2]

He continued discussing the importance of the healthy competition that charters bring to the table. Charter schools are, by design, meant to be innovative and unique, offering families something different.

I really do believe competition is a good thing. And you know the beauty of charters is that if it is not working, for the most part, charters don't survive if they don't have a good product. So that mere fact, charters are always refining themselves so they can be better. You want competition. And it has helped, because of that competition, traditional public schools will be better as well. So I do believe the importance of competition and the importance of being able to cohabitate as organizations.[3]

Escobedo's thoughts echo that of some of the original proponents of the charter school movement. Charters were thought to have the potential, as innovators of education, to influence traditional public schools. It appears that Chula Vista, under the tutelage of Escobedo is doing that very thing. But what has become of the charter he led under the Feaster-Edison name?

"As Escobedo discussed the potential of charter schools development, he discussed the importance of an environment where there is dialogue among leaders."

Led by executive director Francesco Velasco, the school now includes transitional kindergarten through eighth grade with over 1,200 students. Eighty-seven percent of the school's population fall into the category of "socioeconomically disadvantaged." Fifty-six percent are English language learners. The demographics include 91 percent Hispanic, 3 percent white, 2.5 percent black/African American, and a small percentage of American Indian, Alaska Native, Asian, Filipino, or two or more groups.

Feaster Charter School's program still follows some of the tenets of Edison Project's curriculum and philosophy including character education focusing on key areas such as honesty, respect, and responsibility, and a curriculum comprised of classics in literature, science, and the humanities, ninety minutes of daily reading, and daily lessons in music, art, Spanish, and physical education. Located on the same property for over ninety years, the school has grown, adding grade levels, numbers of students, and developing a broader curriculum encompassing twenty-first-century components.

When Francisco Velasco joined the school, he saw even greater potential. With its futuristic vision, he has added several academies within the charter: STEM Academy (science, technology, engineering, and mathematics), VAPA Academy (visual and performing arts), and Feaster Charter Middle's STEAM Academy (science, technology, engineering, arts, and mathematics). In kindergarten, children are exposed to both STEM curriculum and VAPA curriculum. During the elementary years, the students choose either the STEM or VAPA curriculum. In middle school, qualified students are placed in the STEAM Academy. All students are exposed to both STEM and VAPA curriculums throughout their elementary and middle school years. Each academy has its own separate principal with Velasco at the helm over both.

The school has had an impressive track record since becoming a charter school in 1997. With similar demographics to its early days, it had evolved from one of the lowest performing schools in the district to one of the highest; however, Velasco was determined to continue to improve the outcome for the students. He quickly realized the importance of adding to the K–6 configuration and increasing the focus on twenty-first-century skills.

CORPORATE PARTNERSHIPS

Today Feaster includes transitional kindergarten through eighth grade, proudly carrying forward its legacy and traditions, but also partnering with others to be on the cutting edge of innovation. Each academy forms partnerships and builds competencies in relevant areas while continuing to address building character.

The STEM and STEAM academies, through partnerships with local corporations, prepare students for careers in the growing technology industry. In 2015, Feaster Charter School won the INSPIRE Award for its innovative engineering lab, "Maker Lab." With its own engineering curriculum aligned with Common Core and Next Generation Science standards written by school personnel, Feaster tackles a trend they saw with their students: difficulty persevering through the process of identifying and solving problems.

Through hands-on experiences, students learn engineering principles. The engineering lab was created in partnership with a local company, Qualcomm. Since the early days of Feaster, partnerships have been essential. Since the original Edison partnership, community partnerships have proved to be a big component of Feaster's success.

UNIVERSITY PARTNERSHIPS

Another partnership with San Diego State University's Compact for Success program provides a pathway for Feaster middle school students to attend college. The university provides field trips, creates project opportunities related to university work, and opens the discussion about college admission with Feaster families. Middle school students participate in career fairs to learn about different fields of study. When students graduate from high school, they are guaranteed acceptance if they meet the requirements.

Partnerships like these have led to national recognition. In 2017, Feaster was one of nineteen schools nationwide to be named a 2016–2017 exemplar school by the Partnership for 21st Century Learning. More recently, the school was honored as an Apple Distinguished School for its innovative use of iPad devices in kindergarten through eighth-grade classrooms. Partnerships, community involvement with programs, and providing opportunities have helped shape Feaster into the innovative, student-focused school it is today. In addition, Feaster's success has influenced the district as a whole. STEM, STEAM, and VAPA programs have become an important part of several additional district schools. The district as a whole benefits from local community partnerships.

> **"The school has had an impressive track record since becoming a charter school in 1997. With similar demographics to its early days, it had evolved from one of the lowest performing schools in the district to one of the highest; however, Velasco was determined to continue to improve the outcome for the students."**

Francisco Escobedo's idea of the importance of healthy competition and cohabitation between charter schools and traditional schools within the district seems to be working in Chula Vista, California.

NOTES

1. Fransisco Escobedo, Personal interview via phone, December 17, 2015.
2. Ibid.
3. Ibid.

Chapter 9

Shared Pain

The Story of Orange Grove Elementary

Larry DiCenzo, the principal at Orange Grove Elementary School in Charleston, South Carolina, who led the conversion to charter process, faced an interesting challenge in 2006. Having moved from the northeast to South Carolina, he relied upon his experience as an educational administrator to lead his school while he learned the nuances of his new state and district. During that time, he discovered a resource allocation disparity that created issues for his teachers and his students. Each district school was ranked in a points system that permitted them to hire certain staff, and that ranking was based upon academic performance. In other words, if you led a better performing school, then you lost points that went to a poorer performing school.

While he did not disagree with the system in theory, he noticed a disturbing trend: the struggling schools continued to struggle while the better performing schools had increasing expectations with fewer resources. Larry put it this way, "Our class sizes rose to 30 students, we had less money for supplies, we lost technology, and every year it got worse and worse."[1] As a leader, he knew something had to be done; yet, he did not know what to do until he heard about public school conversion to charter status and started doing his personal research on the matter. Through this research, including the application process and the stakeholder approvals that he realized he had to attain, Larry faced a defining moment.

STRATEGIC PLANNING

Instead of immediately jumping into the conversion cycle, he tried to work within the system to protect the resources needed by his teachers and students. Yet, he exhausted every tool and idea at his disposal, but to no avail. Coming from New Hampshire, where a spirit of independence has been ingrained in its citizenry since the 1700s, he desired to be "in charge of his own destiny." His decision was to pursue public school conversion. When asked about potential disadvantages for conversion, his answer was swift and firm: "None! I saw nothing but advantages." He went on to describe those advantages that focused on two things: allocation and autonomy. In referencing the points system used by his district, Larry said becoming a charter school meant that the school could "allocate our resources to where we saw the greatest need" but, even more important to him, they could "do it quickly."

He understood the political battles and potential struggles of going alone, but he wanted that autonomy. He believed the school could best, at the local level, see the outcomes of their inputs and choose to make the necessary changes.[2] He believed in his people and their vision for their school; so, he approached his school improvement committee (SIC) with the idea. Without dissent, they jumped at the opportunity to become masters of their own destiny.

"His decision was to pursue public school conversion. When asked about potential disadvantages for conversion, his answer was swift and firm: 'None! I saw nothing but advantages.' He went on to describe those advantages that focused on two things: allocation and autonomy."

With the differing stakeholders needing to grant at least two-thirds approval, Larry leveraged the SIC to help with the presentation to their staff. The initial meeting explained all the details but, due to misinformation about the charter sector, became particularly focused on defining what a charter school is and is not. He prepared for any and all questions, but the biggest component was the proposed budget.

The staff immediately saw the benefit of autonomy in resource allocation in three areas: (1) class size reduction, (2) supply money return, and (3) new teacher recruitment (particularly technology and foreign-language teachers). After the preparation and the meeting, the vote occurred with "all but two people" agreeing to the conversion.[3] With the first hurdle cleared, the SIC stressed quiet about this vote because they feared repercussions from the district—namely, that their beloved principal would be removed from the school—and, collectively, the school prepared the charter application for submission.

Once the charter application had been completed, the school scheduled its all-important parent meeting. This sequence of events had a logical plan behind it, which likely led to its success—once the staff bought into the idea and prepared the application, then parents could hear a unified voice on the conversion proposal. The meeting notification simply stated it "was a very important meeting for the future of Orange Grove Elementary" and a packed house turnout occurred.

LEADERSHIP MATTERS

All questions were answered but Larry said that one took him by surprise: "This all sounds great but what happens if you leave?" He committed right then to "stay at least until the Charter was up for renewal" which was five years in the future.[4] He said the crowd "broke into applause" and that response gave the staff hope for a positive outcome in the vote. Instead of holding the vote immediately, they wanted families to have an opportunity to ponder and ask any additional questions; so, the vote was scheduled the following day. Fortunately for Larry, the two-thirds threshold was met with ease; thus, the application was formally completed, signed, and submitted both to the district and the state's charter authorizing entity.

The deliberate process helped the school meet both stakeholder approval thresholds, but it had another, more personal effect. On Friday afternoon, May 26, 2006, Larry received a devastating phone call: his son, an army captain, died from wounds sustained by a roadside bomb in Iraq. He composed himself and left school early, which he never did, so school staff realized something bad occurred.

When they finally heard about the tragedy, school staff spoke openly with comments like these: "We are family, and this is a family loss" and "We share his pain, and we'll pull him up."[5] On Tuesday following the Memorial Day weekend, he returned to school and many questioned why he was there. His response was simple: "The school was part of my family and I needed them too."[6] Without a doubt, the school's charter conversion application created a stronger bond within the school that helped sustain them through personal tragedy. This scene shows the powerful effect of positive school culture when the time is taken to cultivate it.

"Without a doubt, the school's charter conversion application created a stronger bond within the school that helped sustain them through personal tragedy. This scene shows the powerful effect of positive school culture when the time is taken to cultivate it."

REFLECTING ON THE PROCESS

When asked to reflect upon the process and whether he would have done anything differently, Larry paused but said he did the best that he could do.

He believed the school "took the right steps and the success of the school proves it." He added some words of caution for any schools seeking to convert an existing school, and that warning goes back to the autonomy of the school. While the autonomy is a wonderful thing, it does come with a high cost that leaders must be prepared to pay. He said, "The principal needs to know how much work it is. . . . Even though I am a huge fan of charter schools, I will be the first to tell you that all principals are not capable of running a charter school."[7]

He said a strong charter school principal must be willing to work long hours (up to seventy hours a week in the initial years), accept total responsibility for all decisions (there is no central office to blame), and manage finances without district support. This latter reason—budgeting—is one of the most common reasons that charter schools cease to exist.[8] As Larry put it, "If you go bankrupt, you no longer have a school and just did a huge disservice to your students, parents, staff, and community."[9] Despite the challenges, he believed this school leadership position was the most rewarding he ever held.

"He said a strong charter school principal must be willing to work long hours (up to seventy hours a week in the initial years), accept total responsibility for all decisions (there is no central office to blame), and manage finances without district support."

FACILITY ADVANTAGE

One advantage that Larry DiCenzo did not mention is that the facility conveyed with the school through the conversion process while ownership was retained by the school district—now the school's authorizing entity. As such, the conversion removed a major barrier that most charter schools face—facility acquisition and upkeep. In 2009, this facility advantage became even sweeter as the district constructed a brand-new $22.3 million building—"the first that a South Carolina school district has built and designed specifically for a charter school."[10]

While the relationships may have initially been strained between the charter school and its district, time and effort repaired them to the point that both sides worked together in the construction of the new school. The charter school's leaders offered design ideas and feedback prior to construction including "green features" to diminish its environmental impact and air scrubbing machines that should "cut down on sickness and fatigue among students and faculty." Even further, the facility was designed in such a way to become a true community facility—staying open after hours—and the design reflected those features as well.[11]

"While the relationships may have initially been strained between the charter school and its district, time and effort repaired them to the point that both sides worked together in the construction of the new school."

A recurrence of this capital windfall is unlikely due to changes in the South Carolina charter school code. Specifically, Section 59.40-100(A)(2) now includes language requiring approval by "a majority vote of the local school board of trustees" for a school using a facility with "outstanding general obligation bonds debt owed on it" to convert to charter status.[12] Simply put, Orange Grove Elementary Charter School is a one of a kind school that continues to do great things for its students.

LEADERSHIP BEYOND THE SCHOOLHOUSE

Due to the successful public school conversion and school's continued achievement, Larry DiCenzo was placed upon the South Carolina Charter School Advisory Board. This volunteer group reviewed charter applications and recommended them to authorizers for approval. When asked what he looked for in a successful conversion application, he said three things: the principal, the budget, and support.

Larry shared a few examples of more recent conversions and talked through how schools in small, rural communities stepped forward to break away from their districts. He said the successful ones had complete support "where small towns banded together to support them. We were always impressed with that kind of support."[13] If a school had met the stakeholder threshold marks and gained specific support of the town, then it spoke of potential to overcome any economic depression that could hit that area.

"When asked what he looked for in a successful conversion application, he said three things: the principal, the budget, and support. Larry shared a few examples of more recent conversions and talked through how schools in small, rural communities stepped forward to break away from their districts."

The other two points—principal and budget—are interrelated and should be considered as such. As Larry put it, "Everything revolves around the principal and they have to be strong to handle it." He also mentioned a state difference that prepared him for the conversion. While a principal in New Hampshire, he had to prepare his budget, write his grants, and manage the finances independently; however, in South Carolina most of those actions were performed through a district office.

Knowing that most principals lacked that level of budgetary expertise, he, as a board member, checked proposed budgets very carefully and diligently looked at the performance of consulting firms—if one were selected. He said that his "biggest fear from day one was going bankrupt," so he had to press principals to gain confidence that they could deliver what they were promising.[14] In summary, all authorizers have the responsibility to scrutinize both the plan and the people involved with the plan. After all, if the plan is right but the people are wrong, then even the best plan can fail. Chapter 10 highlights this principle.

NOTES

1. Larry DiCenzo, "Re: Charter Conversion and Thank You." Message to Joel Medley, October 2, 2018. Email.
2. Ibid.
3. Ibid.
4. Ibid.
5. Reprint of Diane Knich story, "Road bomb in Iraq Kills Principal's Son" in *The Post and Courier*, accessed on October 19, 2019, at https://www.landstuhlhospitalcareproject.org/douglas-dicenzo/.
6. Larry DiCenzo, Personal interview via phone, October 16, 2019.
7. Ibid.
8. Letter entitled "Nationwide Audit of Oversight of Closed Charter Schools," dated September 28, 2018, by Bryon S. Gordon to Deputy Secretary Mitchell Zais, U.S. Department of Education accessed on October 12, 2019, from https://www2.ed.gov/about/offices/list/oig/auditreports/fy2018/a02m0011.pdf.
9. Personal correspondence between DiCenzo and Medley.
10. Diette Courrege, "Different than Most," accessed on November 16, 2019, from https://www.postandcourier.com/news/different-than-most/article_64d001b4-6913-5f17-934c-8721ea9e1a23.html.
11. Ibid.
12. South Carolina Code of Laws, "Title 59, Chapter 40," accessed on October 12, 2019, from https://www.scstatehouse.gov/code/t59c040.php.
13. DiCenzo, Personal Interview.
14. Ibid.

Chapter 10

A 100-Year Love Story

By John Betterton

John Betterton has served as an educator for 45 years; as a teacher, a counselor, and an administrator. He began his career in a segregated black school in the south, and, for the last thirty years, he served as principal of Bethel Hill School.

HISTORY

There is a small rural community in North Carolina near the Virginia border that has had a love affair with its school for a hundred years. This community is called Bethel Hill. Around 1919 Moses Jones, a local farmer, saw the need for a public school in this small community. He donated approximately twelve acres of his farm on which to build a public school. He also had a portable saw mill brought on site to saw the logs that went into building the school. Other family members and members of the community prepared meals for the workers as they built the school. The simple two-story building contained eight classrooms and an office space. The school operated as part of the Person County public school system serving grades one through eleven for many, many years.

GROWTH AND CHANGE

In later years, grade twelve was added as well as additional buildings to handle the increase in student population. An agriculture building was added to teach the aspiring farmers and eventually the addition of an auditorium showcased the talent of budding performers. The high school sports teams played many teams in their humble facilities but did so with pride. The local medical doctor took particular interest in broadening the horizons of the rural student population and worked to expose students to other cultures besides their own. Overall, Bethel Hill was considered the jewel in the middle of the tobacco fields in this rural part of North Carolina.

Fast forward to the 1960s when the school experienced the integration and consolidation of public schools like so many other American public schools during that decade. As a result of consolidation several small schools in the county were closed, but Bethel Hill was spared. While seemingly a blessing at the time, this act would later come back to haunt the Bethel Hill community.

One immediate change was that Bethel Hill School was reconfigured to house grades kindergarten through sixth grade. Several of the buildings which had been designed specifically for high school students were completely abandoned. As was the case in many rural areas during this time, the population in rural areas did not grow as much as the urban areas, and the school reflected that in its enrollment. Bethel Hill had become one of the smaller schools in the system.

By 1987 the issue of closing the school came up for consideration by the Person County Board of Education due to its small size and outdated facility. The groundswell of Bethel Hill parents and Person County citizens shocked everyone. On March 3 of that year the local board held a hearing in the county auditorium. The auditorium filled to capacity and the community members strongly voiced their objection to closing the school. The parents wrote articles in the local paper, made and posted signs along the highway, and conducted a public relations campaign to keep the school open.

> **"As a result of consolidation several small schools in the county were closed but Bethel Hill was spared. While seemingly a blessing at the time, this act would later come back to haunt the Bethel Hill community."**

On March 24 the local board held an official meeting in the Superior Courtroom to vote on the closing issue. Again the parents and citizens filled the courtroom to view the vote. The courtroom was quiet as the Board of Education began their deliberations. The board, perhaps intimidated by the strong community turnout, eventually voted to keep the school open, but noted many deficiencies with the existing facility. The community and school could not be discouraged; they had "dug in" to continue their love relationship with Bethel Hill. The battle was contentious and left many scars on both sides of the issue. However, the community held fast and the superintendent later said he would never recommend closing Bethel Hill again.

POLITICAL CHALLENGES

Fast forward again to 1999 when the superintendent proposed a bond referendum to improve elementary facilities for the county elementary schools.

Several of the local government officials were from the communities where schools had been closed in the 1960s. Rather than send funds to other elementary schools, they used their positions to pressure the School Board to close Bethel Hill. The proposed referendum appeared to be designed in a manner to intentionally anger much of the citizenry in the county. The referendum included funding to build a new classroom facility at Bethel Hill at the expense of construction projects at other elementary schools that were also direly needed.

The plan worked as the bond referendum failed. The Person County Board of Education used this as its motivation to attempt to close Bethel Hill School again. On June 11, 2000, Bethel Hill was intended to close its doors to educating the children of this still rural community forever. It was the last day of school, fifth grade students were holding their annual graduation ceremonies, and the parents filled the school's auditorium. In an act of showing the finality of this decision, the superintendent had U-Haul trucks parked in the school parking lot, ready to load all of the furniture from all of the buildings as the students marched out of the auditorium one last time. It was a sad and bitter scene and a general sense of hopelessness prevailed.

A LIGHT IN THE DARK

After a few weeks of mourning over the closure, the Bethel Hill parents and community leaders found a new reason not to give up entirely on their school. They learned about the North Carolina charter school conversion process and immediately began exploring all possible options to reopen the newly closed school. The Bethel Hill parents and community leaders, who were mostly farmers, began the long journey of changing their beloved traditional public school to a public charter school.

For months they met to investigate the application process. First, as a requirement of the application they had to survey the present parents to see if they supported the conversion of Bethel Hill Elementary into a public charter school. A minimum of 60 percent approval was required, and they quickly received 85 percent.

With that data in hand they began completing various parts of the application. They had to select a curriculum, establish a business plan, design an educational plan, and select a governing board. This group of founders felt that the state health and retirement plan was too expensive, so they decided to create their own, and as they soon found out, there were definite advantages to their plan. Teachers could retire from the North Carolina plan with thirty years of service and then begin teaching at Bethel Hill Charter without penalty. This fact became a strong point for parents as the school was able to attract veteran teachers to their "new" school.

"The Bethel Hill parents and community leaders, who were mostly farmers, began the long journey of changing their beloved traditional public school to a public charter school."

The group also had to come up with a curriculum. This was an entirely new experience for most of the group. Someone discovered the Core Knowledge curriculum that covered all of the traditional subjects and appeared to be highly respected in educational circles. Consequently, they adopted the Core Knowledge curriculum.

Finally, the Bethel Hill board of directors were named, and the charter application was ready for delivery to the Office of Charter Schools at the North Carolina Department of Public Instruction.

Eventually, the Bethel Hill Board and other interested community people traveled to Raleigh and presented their application before the Charter School Review Committee. The community was notified in December of 1999 that their application had received a positive review and that a formal decision would be made in February of 2000 at the State Board meeting. The excitement felt by this small group of committed people that had accomplished such a feat on their own was openly expressed in the community.

A NEW BEGINNING

Bethel Hill did indeed receive a charter at that meeting and was approved to open the upcoming August 2000. To further deepen the meaning of the event, the approved charter was officially presented to the new Bethel Hill Charter School Board Chairman, Joe Berryhill, grandson of Moses Jones. But there was little time for reveling in their success. Now the *real* work would begin.

The first big hurdle was securing a facility. Obviously the stakeholders wanted to stay in the Bethel Hill community, but there were no possible plausible facilities there except the existing school building. Even though that facility had not been maintained properly for thirty years, the parents approached the local Board of Education about the possibility of using the existing facility. Perhaps out of remorse for this community combined with key community leaders calling in favors, the Person County Board of Education agreed to lease the property to the "new" school "as is" for $1 a year.

"But there was little time for reveling in their success. Now the real work would begin."

The parents began basic improvements to the facility immediately. The list of needs was long. The water lines leaked, the sewer system was out of compliance, there was no furniture, paint was peeling, sinks had been taken out, there were no books or instructional materials, and school started in six weeks. An outpouring of parents and friends showed up at night and on weekends to do whatever work that was necessary to make the facility usable for the upcoming school year. Even grandparents got into the act by volunteering their time.

"Perhaps out of remorse for this community combined with key community leaders calling in favors, the Person County Board of Education agreed to lease the property to the 'new' school 'as is' for $1 a year."

As the hot summer days arrived, the work not only continued but accelerated. With the first hurdle secured and renovations well underway, they moved to the second major hurdle of opening a school, securing students and staff. Enrollment forms were widely distributed to Bethel Hill students as well as all other students in the county. By July 1 there were 217 students scheduled to attend the new Bethel Hill Charter School in August.

Even with this enrollment list, there was some uneasiness because some were skeptical as to the full intent on the part of the students and parents; the nagging question lingered in the background, would they all come through in August? Families were being asked to return to an old building versus going to a brand, new fancy building elsewhere.

LEADERSHIP MATTERS

But they all showed up! In retrospect, perhaps it was due to their chosen leader. In the month of April, before the closing of Bethel Hill School, the new Bethel Hill Charter Board realized that they had to hire a leader. To do this, they turned to the prior Bethel Hill Elementary school principal who had moved on to a district position following the school's closing. His love for the school equaled the community's, and he accepted their offer to officially leave his district work to begin his "new" job on July 1.

He immediately began working on charter business at night in the community college small business center while continuing to fulfill his duties with Person County Schools during the day. Miraculously, all fourteen teaching positions and six teacher assistant positions for the new charter school were filled by August. Other support positions were filled as well, and all were eager to get started.

The third hurdle for the group (at this point these hurdles were occurring simultaneously) was acquiring the needed furniture and instructional material with very few funds. Once again, the community was mobilized and contact was made with numerous public school system surplus warehouses, local industries, and nearby universities and a multitude of yard sales were visited.

The parents hit a gold mine when they contacted Wake County Public Schools surplus. Wake County quoted a price of $300 per "truck load" of their surplus materials. The parents got a big farm truck and collected enough student desks for the entire school. Furniture was stacked as high as possible with some tied to the sides of the truck. Some said they looked like Jed Clampet and the Beverly Hillbillies coming through town.

A local industry that had recently closed was contacted by some parents and they donated enough office desks for the teachers. However, all of this furniture had been stored in dirty warehouses and was in need of serious deep cleaning. One of the parents had connections at Duke University and was able to secure used bookcases, tables, and office chairs at a nominal cost. More parents came in and worked for weeks cleaning and removing old gum from the used student desks. By mid-August the student desks and the teacher desks were clean and in place for faculty to teach and students to learn.

"The parents got a big farm truck and collected enough student desks for the entire school. Furniture was stacked as high as possible with some tied to the sides of the truck. Some said they looked like Jed Clampet and the Beverly Hillbillies coming through town."

ANCILLARY CONSIDERATIONS

The fourth hurdle was figuring out how to transport the students, and the fifth was finding ways to feed them as well. With all of the pressing issues and lack of adequate time for strategic planning, the board decided to contract out the food service and transportation function for the new school.

A private company was contracted to supply the buses and run the routes. Unfortunately, the board learned a quick and painful lesson when the transportation company did not deliver as promised. Their unreliability caused the board to quickly terminate the contract in favor of providing student transportation themselves. Several of the board members went to area school systems and purchased surplus buses to use. The buses were cleaned up, drivers were assigned, routes were created, and the school took on the function of transporting the students themselves.

The cafeteria building in the school had been stripped bare by the public school system, even to the sinks on the wall, so operating a cafeteria on site was out of the question. A local caterer agreed to provide lunches for the students at low cost. The catering contract also proved to be a challenge due to the lack of dependability. Eventually the school was able to purchase necessary equipment to begin serving lunch prepared on campus.

After all of the major hurdles were cleared, school started on time in mid-August of 2000 as planned. The school started with 217 students and fully staffed. The campus was old, but to the Bethel Hill folks it was beautiful. Near the end of the first year the Bethel Hill Board wanted to make significant improvements, so they approached the Person County Board of Education about purchasing the property. Several members said sure, but they wanted a million dollars for the facility. After some contentious negotiations and calling in some favors the figure of $300,000 was agreed upon.

The first project was to renovate the abandoned agriculture building that had not been used for almost fifty years. The old shop was redesigned to house three kindergarten classes, one central area, and bathrooms. Using community volunteers and prison inmate labor the building was renovated and ready for students in August. Six weeks later an application for a federal grant came in the mail from North Carolina Department of Public Instruction providing from $50,000 to $500,000 to improve public school facilities.

The grant was applied for with the hope of at least getting $50,000. Much to the surprise and joy the school got the full $500,000 grant. This grant enabled the school to renovate the school's cafeteria, auditorium, and a classroom building built in 1925. The 1925 classroom building had to be redesigned as well to accommodate grades three and four.

The student population grew rapidly and a long waitlist quickly formed. There was pressure from parents to accept more students. The Bethel Hill Board decided to build an additional classroom building for grades one and two. To accomplish this they applied for and received a USDA loan. The building was built by the end of the third year; however, the demand continued to grow and again there was pressure to expand after year four.

The Bethel Hill Board approached the owner of the farm adjacent to the school's property about purchasing several acres. He was not interested in several acres but would sell the entire farm of sixty-plus acres. The board bought the farm and began to make plans for expansion but had to delay the plans due to lack of funds. The school operated at a capacity of 300 students for several more years, and each year prospective parents would leave the enrollment lottery disappointed and in tears.

"After all of the major hurdles were cleared, school started on time in mid-August of 2000 as planned. The school started

with 217 students and fully staffed. The campus was old but to the Bethel Hill folks it was beautiful."

On Saturday, April 15, 2011, disaster struck. A tornado touched down in Person County, and Bethel Hill Charter School got a direct hit that afternoon. Within an hour first responders arrived on scene and blocked the campus off to the public. They did allow the school's leadership on site to assess the damage.

Almost all buildings had damage with shingles off of roofs, windows broken, air conditioner units dangling from rooftops, trees twisted, power lines down everywhere, but most of the damage was to the gym. The roof was taken off of the gym and was laying in the middle of the highway. Nothing could be done at that point because it was beginning to get dark. Sunday morning approximately thirty community people were on campus with tractors, trucks, hand tools, chain saws, and other equipment needed for cleanup and repair.

"However, facility and student growth is not the whole story. The preparation of the Bethel Hill students to be successful in pursuing their dreams is the real story. Many of the students have chosen to continue their education at the university level or community college while others have entered the military or directly into the world of work."

Fortunately the next week was spring break for the students, so they had one week to get the campus back together. Every day during the week a large group would show up and pitch in and by the following Monday most everything was back in place to have school. The students did not miss a single day of school.

Several years later the school became the benefactor of a major financial gift. One alumnus of Bethel Hill School who had left the area to pursue his career and was very successful left a major part of his estate to the school. With those funds the school was able to build another classroom building and add to the infrastructure to accommodate 400 students. Beginning in 2013 the school was able to enroll 400 students and still had a wait-list. However, facility and student growth is not the whole story. The preparation of the Bethel Hill students to be successful in pursuing their dreams is the real story. Many of the students have chosen to continue their education at the university level or community college while others have entered the military or directly into the world of work.

It has been 100 years since Moses Jones cut down the first tree to build a school in the Bethel Hill community. It has been twenty years since the people in the community stepped forward to save the school from demolition. As a result the school and community will be positioned to continue their love story for another 100 years.

Chapter 11

What If?

A History of the Learning Center! Charter School

By Mary Jo Dyre

Mary Jo Dyre began her career in education as a teacher in the 1970's in the Mississippi Delta. This lead her to The Learning Center from 1983–1997, and then through the private conversion to a North Carolina Public Charter School from 1997 through to the present.

"What if?" is such a simple question, yet a powerful one. This short query, made up of two words, with a grand total of six letters in the entire question, however, has been the driving force behind my long history with the Learning Center, 1983–1997, and through the private conversion to a North Carolina Public Charter School, 1997 through the present. Being open to the "What if?" question has continuously molded and shaped the school, never allowing us to sit stagnant, always forcing yet more questions to be asked. The willingness to ask "What if?" has sustained a focus on education that remains both alive and vibrant.

FROM TEACHER (AND MOTHER) TO TEACHER LEADER

I knew early that I wanted to be an educator. My fifth grade teacher had opened my eyes to the possibility that can unfold in a classroom. A junior high school language arts teacher sealed the deal by instilling in me a love of literature. Never questioning my career decision, both undergraduate and graduate studies moved me closer to my professional plans. My first two years in the classroom, 1976–1978, took place at Quitman County High School in the Mississippi Delta.

As a 1970 high school graduate in Mississippi, I had lived through the challenging transition of integration. I was one who had chosen to stay with the newly integrated public schools. When it came time to sign my first teaching contract, I did not hesitate to work in the public school system. I was not drawn to the private schools that were brought into existence to avoid integration. With this particular history under my belt, what led to eventually founding a private school in 1983?

"I soon realized I was selling a dream each and every time I talked to prospective backers, teachers and prospective parents."

Marriage, the birth of one child, and a move to North Carolina in the midst of expecting a second child produced a major paradigm shift in my world as I focused on the very fulltime job of motherhood. Still an educator at heart, I was intent on giving my children the best during these very formative years. I do not think I will ever forget recognizing my daughter's first signs of wanting something more than I was offering in the home. What was I missing? Was it more socialization, or possibly a preschool setting that was rich in hands-on activities? Trying a local day care setting a couple of mornings a week soon led me to more research.

THE MAGIC OF MONTESSORI

As it turned out, the nearby town of Murphy had a Montessori preschool that met in the back of the Episcopal Church. The more I learned about Maria Montessori's philosophy the more I became convinced that every child should be exposed to a rich learning environment where a large offering of activities is available, within a setting specially designed for a young learner. The teacher should ideally serve as a facilitator for learning and discovery.

Unfortunately, I found out early during the 1982 enrollment process that this Montessori program had plans to close by the end of the school year. Initially, I saw no options of choice for my daughter's education. That was the moment when I first looked the possibility square in the eye and asked, "What if? What if I started a school based on the Montessori method?"

If I had known more about starting a business and the challenges of running a private school in an economically deprived section of the Appalachian Mountains, I may never have opened the school. If I had thought through more carefully what I was trying to start with only a year and a half to bring the project from initial inspiration to the grand opening for a first day of school, I would have conceded defeat within the first couple of months. Instead, I focused on what I defined as the ideal approach to education.

I ate, drank, and dreamed the vision. I began to gather like-minded people around my idea of providing a choice in education. Two of my colleagues at Tri-County Community College, Cherokee County, NC, took to the road to visit other schools for ideas. We went to the big city of Atlanta where the Yellow Pages had lists and lists of interesting schools to explore. We headed out together in a yellow Volkswagen, parking alongside the fine cars that often had nannies dropping off students in some of Atlanta's most elite private schools. We were on a mission. We walked in with heads held high, intent on finding what constituted the best of education.

Montessori continued to win hands down. "What if?" consumed me every waking moment. What if we could bring back home some of the ideas we were seeing? What if I could pick up the Montessori materials from the little school that would soon be closing? What if I could not find Montessori trained teachers in the far west mountains of North Carolina? The "yeas" continued to balance out the challenges of the "nays."

"I ate, drank, and dreamed the vision. I began to gather like-minded people around my idea of providing a choice in education."

CORRALLING COMPLEX CHALLENGES THROUGH CREATIVITY

More tough challenges than just choosing a curriculum rolled in like tidal waves. Where could we find a building with basically no start-up capital? I knew we could never charge the tuition rates we had seen in the posh Atlanta schools. Could we settle on a per-student cost that would pay teachers, buy educational materials, secure a building, and keep the power going each month?

I soon realized I was selling a dream each and every time I talked to prospective backers, teachers, and prospective parents. The Learning Center, located on Green Cove Road, in Brasstown, North Carolina, officially opened its doors in August of 1983, as a Montessori preschool–K and a combination of first–third grade program in a church building. I had found enough fellow dreamers to announce a cry that has been heard continuously from 1983 through the present, "Let's have school!"

The private school years were both exhilarating and challenging. Facility needs moved us to four different locations: first, the dissolution of the church where we were initially holding school; the second site, a former public school that proved impossible financially to renovate (never mind the location just not being ideal for future growth); a third facility that we quickly outgrew once we moved the school into the town of Murphy, North Carolina; and then on to the fourth location that we would eventually outgrow once we became a charter school.

The economic struggles so prevalent in the mountain counties that we served during this timeframe threatened our very existence more than once. It took a great deal of creativity to achieve that delicate balance of charging a tuition rate that enabled us to run a school without out-pricing many of the families that were interested in our approach to education.

Fortunately, we were experiencing daily victories in the classrooms. Year after year, the hands-on, teacher-as-facilitator approach was producing classes of eager, young learners. Although we certainly tried a variety of curriculum with our first–sixth grade students, our richest educational experiences continued to be what would now be called project-based learning.

Although budget constraints certainly dictated combined-grade classrooms, our belief in the Montessori mixed-age approach to learning often saw a first grader sitting in on and comprehending a fourth-grade math lesson. Inviting people from the greater community of learners into our classrooms was a norm. We borrowed, researched, and created materials in an open-source manner, simply seeking out the best information to put in front of our students. "What if?" continued to be asked. We used the world of nature as a classroom. We, against all odds, found ways to include music, the visual arts, and the performing arts.

THE QUESTION MEETS AN ANSWER

It was in this educational setting of daily problem solving and collaboration that "What if?" eventually met the right opportunity as the Charter School Act of North Carolina was ratified in 1996. A cap of 100 charters was set at that time. Thirty-four charter schools opened for the 1997–1998 school year. The Learning Center! Charter School was one of that first round of charter schools that opened up the possibility of a choice in public education in our state.

The group of parents and educators who had worked through the successful charter application process was motivated by the idea that becoming a charter public school would remove the tuition barrier for a geographical area that remains to this day as an economically challenged region.

We were eager to learn all that we could about traditional school expectations and standards. We stayed equally committed to a basic concept of schooling where students were continually engaged in meaningful work. Teachers as facilitators continued as our ideal. Instruction continued to be designed to target diverse needs for a diverse population of learners. We soon realized in those early years as a charter school that there was still very little money for the extras.

Again "What if?" pushed us ahead. "What if" we found community and parent volunteers? "What if" we learned more about grants? "Learning on the run" described our work as we took baby steps toward federal monies that were available and began to explore the idea of offering a school nutrition program. There was so much to learn. In those early charter years, the Department of Public Instruction was, in many ways, learning right along beside us. We asked plenty of questions. We also got the answers we needed to keep our forward momentum.

"It was in this educational setting of daily problem solving and collaboration that 'What if?' eventually met the right opportunity as the Charter School Act of North Carolina was ratified in 1996."

CONNECTING WITH OTHER CHARTERS

Charter leaders began to emerge, an association was formed. Eventually the Office of Charter Schools was created. In those first ten years we often drove six hours both to and from Raleigh for a two-hour meeting. Our closest charter neighbors remained two hours away. We reached for every opportunity we could find in the midst of the annual cry of "Let's have school!" We worked to stay connected to the vision of choice that North Carolina charters had the potential of offering.

We worked equally hard to know what was expected of us from the state level. We remained relentless with asking questions of every division of the Department of Public Instruction. Finding the resource of Acadia Northstar moved us ahead light-years with the ongoing need for support.

I chuckle as I remember when some of our required trainings moved to Charlotte, a town considered more accessible to the western region. I actually smiled when more meetings and trainings began to be offered in Asheville. And, yes, I rejoiced when our most recent annual charter school conference was held in our home county of Cherokee. Continuously improved access to effective technology has played a major role in closing the geographical gap between far west and the rest of the state.

The early 2000s produced continued growth in our student population as our student numbers had doubled at this point, from 65 to around 120. When it became evident that we were outgrowing our fourth location in the Valley Village Shopping Center, we began to work with USDA and local

Macon Bank to obtain direct loans for property and facility. Asking plenty of questions until we found answers that moved us forward produced an amazing result; in approximately ten months, we found a day care to take over our then-existing lease, completed applications and obtained the loans necessary to purchase property. We now have a facility of modules set up. Although we had to postpone the opening of school for seventeen days to obtain the necessary Certificate of Occupancy (CO) and inspections, be assured the cry of "Let's have school!" was once again heard in mid-September of 2000.

The 945 Conaheeta location in Murphy, NC, houses a vibrant educational K–8 charter program that in some ways has not changed its basic approach to education since 1997, the opening year. Our campus also includes a private Montessori preschool.

We are still advocates of hands-on learning; still adhere to the basic premise that every student has potential when met where they are with an approach that reaches each unique learning approach. We still seek teachers who are facilitators. We continue to grow in our appreciation of the power of the "What if?" to spread throughout our school culture. Nothing is more powerful than hearing our students ask "What if?"

As we have consistently held all of the above sacred, we have also stayed open to growth and change. We live in a world that continues to evolve in unprecedented ways with the ever-changing world of technology. Students of the technology age simply learn differently than earlier students.

REFLECTIONS ON OUR RIDE

Although we cannot fully predict the future these students will face, we believe that collaboration and problem solving will always be necessary tools for society to move forward. Our community of learners has expanded beyond our local borders. Resources for project-based learning are available with the click of a computer key. Our rich, varied base of educational offerings is captured under the E-STEAM umbrella: Entrepreneurship, science, technology, engineering, arts and agriculture, and math. Health and wellness hold equal importance with the E-STEAM umbrella of focus. At our present location, the "What if?" question hit its mark as we now offer a nationally recognized school nutrition program coupled with a physical education program and after-school sports programs.

"We continue to grow in our appreciation of the power of the 'What if?' to spread throughout our school culture. Nothing

is more powerful than hearing our students ask 'What if?' As we have consistently held all of the above sacred, we have also stayed open to growth and change."

Our school culture is alive and growing. The arts remain a priority although funding for such remains a challenge. We are presently becoming immersed in a long-term professional development opportunity with Ben Owens, with PBL Works, to become an official Open Way Learning (OWL) academy. Targeted problem and project-based learning support, as well the development of a working understanding of the OWL elements are goals of this in-depth professional development opportunity.

"Being open to the 'What if?' question has continuously molded and shaped the school, never allowing us to sit stagnant, always forcing yet more questions to be asked. The willingness to ask 'What if?' has sustained a focus on education that remains both alive and vibrant."

As founder of a charter school, with a conversion from private to charter in my history, for a long run of offering a choice in education from 1983 to the present, my advice is straightforward. Surround yourselves with board members, fellow leaders, teachers, staff, community supporters, and visionaries who have the diverse backgrounds, the education, the training, the community experience to ask the "What if?" question and then be willing to ask it again and again.

"What if?" will always require a commitment to then ask enough questions to find the answers to whatever the next challenge is. Collaboration and problem solving are essentials. As I stand at the beginning of a slow retirement from a long, fulfilling career as an educator, I am excited for our school's future. I am training a visionary replacement. Insightful educators and vibrant visionaries keep finding their way to our campus. There really is no conclusion to our school's story, only the necessity to dream the dream and keep asking "What if?"

Chapter 12

An Island Story

INTRODUCTION

Earlier in chapter 9, the story was told of Orange Grove Elementary School and its conversion process within a South Carolina coastal district. The leadership at Orange Grove closely watched how another school—only 10 miles away—moved through the conversion process. They intended to learn from the experience of James Island High School to appraise whether or not to initiate their own conversion journey. As such, the authors believe that the story of James Island should be told in light of how a school can continue to lead the way and remain successful—nearly two decades after the charter conversion process.

WRITTEN BY LAURA L. PACE

With Contributions from Timothy Thorn, Principal, and Deborah Farrell, Guidance Director

Located within the Lowcountry of South Carolina, James Island is not a traditional island; but rather a large area of landmass separated by salt marsh and connected by bridges. This island serves as a bedroom community of Charleston that has seen an increase in population and property values in each of the last several decades. Despite these increases, the geography creates difficulties for families—high insurance rates due to the ever-present threat of hurricanes.

Although a coastal community, James Island is a living dichotomy—very wealthy families skew the median income averages with the existence of large pockets of abject poverty as well. When looking at households that rent rather than own, a very telling figure emerges—62.2 percent of those residents live below the poverty level, many in subsidized housing. Surprisingly, the percentage of residents living in poverty is much higher among the children than in the elderly in James Island. Estimates put poverty rates between 7 percent and 16 percent in high school-aged children.

"She saw the cumbersome regulations at the district level that hampered the school's success, so Dr. Gregory conceived an idea and devised a plan with the school leadership team. She wanted to convert the large school to charter status because more flexibility would help them address the needs of an ever-changing student population."

A public high school located in this region must have the dual ability to meet the rigorous instructional expectations of high socioeconomic families while simultaneously supporting academically challenged students. While James Island High School worked diligently with students at all levels, something—an additional nexus for improvement—was missing. Upon finding the flexibility afforded to the school through charter conversion, this award-winning high school excelled in educating students at both ends of the statistical mean.

IDEA TO CONVERT

James Island High School seemed like a typical suburban high school, but its visionary and extraordinary leader, Dr. Nancy Gregory, wanted more. She saw the cumbersome regulations at the district level that hampered the school's success, so Dr. Gregory conceived an idea and devised a plan with the school leadership team. She wanted to convert the large school to charter status because more flexibility would help them address the needs of an ever-changing student population. Dr. Gregory, over time, intentionally developed strong relationships, both within the community and the Charleston County School District (CCSD). When she approached the district with this novel idea, they were not adamantly opposed to the conversion but, admittedly, had no experience in converting or overseeing a charter school.

Dr. Gregory guided the school through the process with a combination of consensus building, complex negotiations with the current administration and some good old-fashioned elbow grease within the community. In July 2003, JICHS became the nation's largest independent converted charter school in the southeastern United States and, officially, changed its name to James

Island Charter High School (JICHS). After more than a decade and a half, the school continues to successfully serve the diverse needs of its student body through efficiency and innovation.

IMPETUS TO CONVERT

Finances

Prior to the conversion, James Island High School rested at the bottom of the per pupil funding schedule within the district. CCSD had many small schools in relatively rural areas requiring an adjustment to the per student funding model that provided those rural students with the ancillary funding. As a result, James Island received a reduced and more modest per pupil funding. In reflecting on the charter origin, Deborah Farrell, present-day director of Guidance, recounted, "If we converted to charter, we could be better able to meet the needs of our students on James Island. The county's decisions were often based on what is better for the good of all Charleston County, but not necessarily James Island."

Once the conversion received approval, months of negotiations and community grassroots lobbying were ahead to ensure the new charter received all funds due them under the law. A result of those negotiations is the hybrid relationship between the school and the district regarding facility maintenance and improvement funding. Routine maintenance is the responsibility of the charter school, but major maintenance, such as a new roof, is paid through the district. When the school built a new wing, that construction was funded through a government bond issue.

The JICHS administration, however, expressed a desire to add even more space to address student needs; and a compromise was reached. The school simply paid for the extra square footage costs above the bond funding. In the next several years, JICHS will have a new stadium and track built by the district.

Mr. Thorn, the current principal of JICHS, came to James Island from Ohio. He was intrigued with the district-supported charter approach, which was unusual in Ohio, and applied for a job. When hired as the assistant principal, where he served for a year and a half, he committed to learning all aspects of the role. As the JICHS principal accepted a district-level position, Mr. Thorn was promoted due to his knowledge of the school and recently gained expertise in areas like charter school finance. He offers us this explanation regarding the funding for charter schools, "All of the schools participate in a district audit each January or February. Whatever the average that they spend per child district-wide is what every charter school gets." Mr. Thorn then takes those funding figures to budget and allocate it in creative and successful manners. To assist in fiscal management of the nearly $17 million annual budget, the school uses a financial firm to manage their budget and pay their bills. Due to strong budgetary practices, the school possesses a $5 million reserve fund, which is a result of charter school conversion.

Curriculum

While a traditional school, JIHS was subject to the curriculum restrictions of CCSD, which included their textbook choices. For instance, the Algebra teachers were forced to use one of two district-adopted textbooks choices. The school's ideas about other more-meaningful books were not allowed due to CCSD protocols mandating all high schools to use identical textbooks. As a charter school, the administrators wanted, and now have, the freedom to work with the teachers to select appropriate textbooks for their students.

> **"Now, the school affords its students unique, authentic, and relevant learning experiences within a context-rich setting."**

Prior to conversion, Dr. Gregory's vision was to create an IB program at the high-school level, which did not exist in Charleston County. Dr. Gregory knew that instituting such a unique international program would require cooperating with the CCSD, and the district superintendent agreed to support this programmatic development by adding $500,000 of spending for the next five years. Dr. Gregory, knowing the need to have the right people in place, specifically sought Deborah Farrell because of her commitment to international education. Ms. Farrell was excited to find a school that enabled her to work within that passion. Working together, they would create the first and only high school IB program in Charleston County; and this program would help justify the conversion to charter status. A charter school, within its application, must describe a novel approach for students, and the IB program fulfilled that need.

The charter approach also allowed the school to utilize school experiences outside of the classroom that were previously prohibited by district rules and regulations. The school's IB program continues to serve as a perfect example. The IB biology class can attend an extended field trip to Florida to participate in hands-on marine biology experiments. This kind of trip would not have occurred previously due to its proximity to water and the aversion to liability. Now, the school affords its students unique, authentic, and relevant learning experience within a context-rich setting.

Hiring

CCSD regulated allotment of school employees to each school based on an archaic "point" system. This system stipulated that all employees were equally worth one point without any differentiation between a high qualified teacher in a core subject or a janitor. Each year, the district would allot the resources for each school, the number of positions that would be hired, and the pool of candidates from which they would choose. This system did not allow the school to respond to needs identified in school data (e.g., supplementary teachers to work in one-on-one settings to support struggling students).

After the conversion process, Deborah shared a critical difference for the personnel process, "When we went charter, we were able to allocate positions based on the goals set by our Leadership Team, and then interviewed and hired through a school-based committee of people who then made recommendations to our board." This streamlined process allowed James Island to hire the right teachers to fill the right need for the students choosing to be at the charter school. Simply, the local control focused on the immediate student body without following the point system created for a district need.

"Dr. Gregory wanted to continue the mission of James Island High School but within the charter school context—gaining administrative and programmatic freedom from the CCSD funding formulas, curricular restrictions, and bureaucratic red tape."

The local flexibility permits James Island to adjust adeptly as the student needs have shifted. For instance, the school has two full-time nurses, whereas most other schools only have one. Further, the administrators wanted to have a mental health therapist on site to work with students. That position originally started as a one-day-a-week position but has now transitioned into a full-time role. These additional resources for students to receive social and emotional learning support are directly attributed to the flexibility afforded the converted school.

Special Needs

Before the conversion, students with different levels of special needs were shuttled throughout the school district to receive their special education services. Profoundly mentally disabled (PMD) students were bused across town to a high school that had a specialized program for those students. Teachable mentally disabled (TMD) students were bused to other zones that were far from home, which was beneficial for the district but not local constituents. James Island wanted a solution amenable to all stakeholders—students, parents, and school.

> **"Charter conversion allowed these students to be served on-site at their home school, thus saving additional transportation and staffing costs at non-charter school locations."**

Starting the year of the conversion and due to the flexibility in hiring afforded charter schools, the TMD students were kept at JICHS, and a specialized program was started to meet their needs. Shortly thereafter, the PMD students were also kept within the school and not bused out. This modification saved both the district and JICHS resources and met the needs of the students in a more educationally appropriate and family-supportive way. Pre-conversion students were bused, at the district's expense, to a location that could meet their needs. Charter conversion allowed these students to be served on-site at their home school, thus saving additional transportation and staffing costs at non-charter school locations.

New Programs

As a direct result of the conversion, school administrators swiftly created new programs in response to identified local needs. When students were involved in serious behavioral issues that may not merit immediate expulsion, Dr. Gregory and her staff started the "We Care" program. These student cases underwent review by the JICHS Discipline Board who could recommend them to this setting. In a traditional school setting, many more layers would have been in place, such as a board of directors and a superintendent review; however, through flexibility from the charter sphere, the school could make these decisions locally.

If assigned to "We Care," the students shifted from the larger, school setting and were educated for one or two semesters in an adjacent trailer. A highly qualified teacher led the classroom that was capped at no more than twelve students. Further, the school provided daily, specialized transportation from their home directly to their classroom. The program was very successful and permitted students to avoid a permanent expulsion on their school records.

In examining school disciplinary data for programmatic success, JICHS had zero incidents involving firearms, no sexual assaults or physical attacks with weapons, and only one student was expelled during the 2018–2019 school year. However, there were 205 in-school suspensions. These statistics indicate the innovation through local control of the "We Care" program had significant success. On the day of an interview, Mr. Thorn, the principal of the school, added another testament of this success in that he was signing an early graduation permission slip for a participant of the program. The student performed so well that they not only graduated but they graduated early!

ISSUES IN CONVERSION

When the school began its conversion process, smaller charter schools existed within CCSD, but the student target audiences varied widely. Unfortunately, those schools did not offer sustained academic success over time. Dr. Gregory wanted to change that fact by continuing the mission of James Island High School but within the charter school context—gaining administrative and programmatic freedom from the CCSD funding formulas, curricular restrictions, and bureaucratic red tape.

"The process of conversion took approximately eighteen months as these were unchartered political, financial, and legal waters."

When reflecting on this transition Deborah remarked, "I guess I was naive in a lot of ways. I just thought that people were going to do the right thing and be honest and it blew my mind how hard it was. We spent a lot of time in the community because we . . . had to counteract some misinformation that was being shared by a few individuals within the school district." The fear was that the charter school would function more like a selective magnet school and would begin to exclude their traditional neighborhood students. Rumors, focusing on student demographics, became commonplace and alleged that minority students or students with disabilities would no longer be welcome at the school.

The process of conversion took approximately eighteen months as these were unchartered political, financial, and legal waters. The transition period was difficult, both for the high school and the school district, which found themselves at odds despite the common goal of efficiently and effectively educating students. At one point, the district told the James Island teachers that signing pro-charter paperwork would lead to nonrenewal of their contracts. Everyone was stunned. Eventually, the state's attorney general ruled on this disagreement siding with the charter school—teacher stance on the conversion did not affect their contract.

Unfortunately, the angst continued. The district then informed the James Island administration of a major change regarding the facility. If they went charter, then access to the current facility would be forfeited. Again, a legal

Table 12.1 2019 South Carolina Report Cards – High School Point Scale

Excellent	67–100
Good	60–66
Average	51–59
Below average	40–50
Unsatisfactory	39 and below

Table 12.2 Score Comparison Charter Conversion, District, and State

Content Area	James Island (%)	District Average (%)	Points Better than District	State Average (%)	Points Better than State
English	72.6	64.5	8.1	56.3	16.3
Algebra	79.6	63.7	15.9	54.9	24.7
Biology	78.3	64.9	13.4	54.4	23.9
US History	59.1	56.6	2.5	47.7	11.4
English Learners	69.7	47.6	22.1	49.8	19.9
Graduation	91.2	84.2	7	81.1	10.1

NOTE: for the core content areas, the metric considers those scoring a "C" or higher.
All of the data above can be found on the James Island Charter School Report Card accessed at https://www.screportcards.com/overview/?q=eT0yMDE5JnQ9SCZzaWQ9MTAwMTYxNg on January 4, 2019.

clarification had to be made, which was in favor of the charter school keeping the physical plant based upon two factors: (1) the taxpayers had paid for the building, and (2) a previous charter conversion in the upstate of South Carolina had already been permitted to keep their building.

IMPACT OF CONVERSION

School performance data is published by CCSD through "School Report Cards." These metrics offer an overall rating, with the scale listed in table 12.1, based upon the following areas: academic achievement, preparing for success, English learner's progress, graduation rate, and college/career readiness (see table 12.1).

For the 2018–2019 academic year, JICHS scored a 73 placing it in the "excellent" category. This result was five points higher than the year before and tied for the highest score across all CCSD charter schools. When comparing SAT scores across the district, JICHS students performed fourth best of all public schools, with a 1,068 average SAT score. To further show the academic performance of James Island, see the chart in table 12.2 as it compares the charter conversion with both the district and state averages in each category.

Over the past year, JICHS graduates showed a near 7 percent increase in the percentage of students enrolled in a two- or four-year college of technical college pursuing a degree, certificate, or diploma. Specifically, the graduating class could be separated this way: 52 percent attending a four-year college, 33 percent attending a two-year or technical college, 5 percent entering the military, 8 percent joining the workforce, and 2 percent pursing other goals. Almost 47 percent of JICHS graduates qualified for scholarship programs based on grade point averages and test scores. These scholarships range from $2,500 to $7,500 per year, renewable for four years. The scholarships awarded to the class of 2019 graduates, as reported by the time of graduation, was more than $8.5 million dollars.

Perhaps the most visible public measurement of the success of the charter school is that JICHS has deliberately maintained an open-door policy for students who do not reside within the "home school" boundary, as defined by the school district. A lottery system is used to select students who can attend through the school choice application process, and, this past year, nearly 280 out-of-home school district students applied.

While the application number may appear insignificant, it must be understood within this context: CCSD offers multiple options through magnet schools, charter schools, and others. This open-door policy is encouraged by the CCSD because it provides a level of student choice and student access to specialized programs such as the IB program at James Island.

IMPRESSIONS

In hindsight, Dr. Gregory's decision to convert to charter status fundamentally changed Charleston County schools. As with so many other successful conversions, the relationship with the district improved over time, and CCSD has become much more accepting of charter schools. Currently, there are nine charter schools supported by CCSD, serving approximately 4,825 students, of which JICHS serves 1,648 or 34 percent of the charter school population. These charter schools provide students with options that would not have been available to them before the charter conversion process. The district is stronger. The schools are stronger, and the students are reaping the benefits.

Looking back over the past seventeen years since the charter conversion process, James Island has risen above a unique conversion process to become a highly successful and academically challenging educational institution. The continued mission is addressing the diverse needs of its student body population. It was only through conversion that the school could respond quickly and efficiently to implement the right strategies at the right time. The conversion legacy is that students are graduating well equipped with necessary skills to succeed in our modern era.

"The district is stronger. The schools are stronger, and the students are reaping the benefits."

Chapter 13

Legacy of Leadership

The Key to Conversion

Each school and story highlighted in this book showcase a singular, important point—a charter conversion, if done well, can be sustained as a legacy through strong leadership. It has been said that everything rises and falls upon leadership, and charter school conversion (the initial and subsequent processes) is no different. The vitality of leadership resides in the fact that the newly earned flexibility brings absolute accountability for results for better or for worse. The leadership needed to sustain the charter school conversion includes the following strands: financial acumen, instructional expertise, political wisdom, cultural discernment, and community intelligence.

In closing, consider the acronym given in table 13.1 as a summary for a successful and sustained charter school conversion.

Yes, the conversion journey may be arduous; but the reward, for students and staff, is abundant.

Table 13.1 Critical Steps to Conversion

C Comprehend your state's laws, policies, regulations, and application expectations.
O Own your results—all of them.
N Nurture your leadership pipeline with care to effectively manage transitions.
V Validate your mission by every instructional, financial, and personnel decision.
E Expect unplanned issues requiring negotiation and novel solutions.
R Raise community support both inside and outside the school community.
T Take risks to innovate, learn, and share with others.

About the Authors

Rebecca A. Shore is an associate professor in the Department of Educational Leadership at the University of North Carolina at Charlotte. Prior to UNC Charlotte, Dr. Shore worked in schools for twenty-eight years in California, Louisiana, and North Carolina: thirteen years of teaching and fifteen years in school administration. She received an undergraduate degree in Music Education from Louisiana State University, and her doctoral degree in Educational Administration and Policy is from the University of Southern California. She has two grown children and resides with her husband in North Carolina. This book's coauthors, Dr. Leahy and Dr. Medley, are both former students of Dr. Shore.

Maria M. Leahy has been a teacher and administrator in a school specializing in meeting the needs of students with unique learning challenges, chair of a board of directors for a charter school whose mission is to develop health and wellness for mindful citizens, and is currently an administrator in a parochial high school. Dr. Leahy earned her doctorate in Educational Leadership at the University of North Carolina, Charlotte; her dissertation title is "Characteristics and Skills of Sustained Leaders of Successful Public Charter Schools in North Carolina." She has two grown daughters, and her hope is that schools will be places of great joy and learning for her grandchildren and all children.

Joel E. Medley is a native North Carolinian and was taught the importance of education as a child. His father dropped out of high school and ensured that his children would not repeat that mistake. He became the first person in his family to graduate from a four-year college and the first to pursue postgraduate work. He received his bachelor's degree in Social Studies Education from Bob Jones University, where he was named the university's Secondary Student Teacher of the Year. He continued his education at the University of North Carolina at Greensboro completing two master's degrees, and finished with a doctoral degree focused on leadership from a seminary. Dr. Medley has served as a school administrator in both charter and traditional schools. For two years, he led the Charter and Magnet School program for the South Carolina Department of Education. He also served as the director of the NC Office of Charter Schools, an authorizing entity, for five years. Currently, he serves as the director of Leadership Development for school and academic leaders at K12, Inc.

www.ingramcontent.com/pod-product-compliance
Lightning Source LLC
Chambersburg PA
CBHW051814230426
43672CB00012B/2731